SEOUL:
TALE OF A SMART CITY

SEOUL:
TALE OF A SMART CITY

LESSONS FROM SOUTH KOREA ON HOW TO BUILD SMARTER CITIES

KRISTI SHALLA
AND
SUNG JIN PARK

atmosphere press

This book is dedicated to our parents,
PFC Fay Shalla, Hyung-Jun Park and Jeong-Im Chun,
and all the men and women who brought the light to
South Korea. The world is forever in their debt.

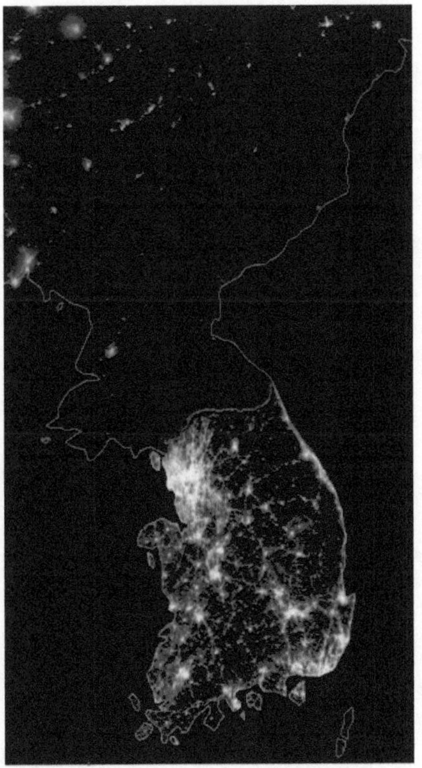

(Source: earthdata.nasa.gov)

Contents

2020 AND BEYOND

APPENDIX

Preface

When Dr. Park and I set out to write this book in 2021, from cities on opposite sides of the planet, our main objective was to create a case study of Korean smart cities that anyone could read. I had been working in the area of transport and smart mobility and saw the effect efficient transport had on people's lives. Living between New York and Barcelona most of my adult life, I had gotten used to reliable and efficient public transportation. When I went to Manila or met people from Latin America and understood the issues they faced in getting around their cities, it made me understand how their transport systems were limiting growth and opportunity.

My 'aha' moment came in 2018 when I met a transport expert from Mexico City who is part of the *Women in Transport* group at the International Transport Forum in Leipzig, Germany. I had been working on a project with the Korea Railroad Research Institute on a predictive tool for public transport management and had learned how many problems existed in the city of Seoul related to the reliability of public transportation in the 1990s, before the system was reformed to become one of the best in the world. In my conversation with the Mexican expert on mobility, I found that the problems she was dealing with in Mexico were exactly the same as Seoul's problems in the 1990s. This is when I first thought that the story of Seoul's smart city development deserved a wider audience.

Dr. Park and I were introduced when conducting research for a different book, *Implementing Data-Driven Strategies in Smart Cities* (Grimaldi & Carrasco-Farré, 2021). She was an expert with over two decades of experience in urban planning and smart city development. Throughout our first conversations, it became clear that we had common interests and common goals. She also believed that the smart city development history of Korean cities could be a meaningful reference for urban policy experts or decision-makers in cities around the world. Since we were both passionate about smart city development as a means of creating more equitable societies, I became convinced that our knowledge was very complementary and that we would be able to produce something meaningful together.

For the book project, we have been meeting on Zoom every week for nearly two years. During this time, we have talked extensively about Korean developmental history and discussed the contribution of urban interventions as well as, of course, the value of different aspects of Korean pop culture. It has been an intensely collaborative and enjoyable partnership. We are very happy to finally present a work that we hope will broaden the global conversation around smart city development.

There has been extensive coverage of smart city development in academia, and much of what we cover in this book is well known among researchers in each individual field. However, little has been written about the combined effects of smart city policies and how they improve the city environment and the lives of residents. We value highly the academics and researchers who deal with these topics and know that their work is integral to creating a basis for policy changes. However, we also know that some people who have the power to effect change in cities are not all trained engineers and scientists and don't usually read academic research. Because smart city development has the potential to significantly impact daily life, this topic needs to be taken into the mainstream. We want to help people understand how smart city policies are really about opportunity, equity and quality of life, and citizen-centered policies are really about bringing users of city services into the conversation.

Seoul's transformation into a smart city is inextricably linked to the nation's history. One of the most enjoyable parts of writing this book was taking a deep dive into South Korea's postwar history. We both had strong ties to the country before we started (especially Dr. Park, who is Korean), but there were holes in our knowledge. We spent a lot of time educating ourselves and each other about South Korea and its development story. This undoubtedly slowed us down but was worthwhile as it elevated the quality of our analysis.

Timelines play a very important role in this book. This story is organized in chronological order. We feel that this is necessary because of the way newer interventions have been built on older ones. The story of shared mobility policy in Chapter 11 can only be told after the story of public transport reforms from Chapter 5. Seoul's beautification story of the riverside area in Chapter 8 is more relevant when the reader understands the pivotal steps taken to bring nature back to the urban center in Chapter 4.

In Chapters 1 and 2, we start with a short history of South Korea and the city of Seoul to better understand the dynamic urban environment that existed before the arrival of the three mayors. In Chapter 3, we start with a description of how Lee Myung-bak came to be the Mayor of Seoul and what influenced him in his policy goals. After that, Chapters 4 and 5 delve into a descriptive analysis of Lee Myung-bak's signature smart city interventions: the Cheonggyecheon Restoration Project and the Seoul Public Transport Reform. In Chapter 6, we build the profile of Oh Se-hoon, and then in Chapter 7 explore his efforts to make Seoul a design capital. In Chapters 8 and 9, we look at Oh Se-hoon's efforts to develop the Han River waterfront area and his affordable housing program. Chapter 10 starts with an overview of Park Won-soon and his journey to first becoming a social activist and then the Mayor of Seoul. In Chapter 11, we describe his vision for Seoul as a sharing city, and then in Chapter 12, we look at his efforts to implement mechanisms for **data-driven decision making**. In Chapter 13, we look at the creation of Seoul Urban Solutions Agency (SUSA), an office created with the goal of sharing Seoul's smart city knowledge with the rest of the world. After that, we wrap the book up with a brief overview of Seoul since 2020 and Oh Se-hoon's new 2030 vision for development.

One of the most challenging parts of writing this book has been skirting political issues. Because we wanted this work to have a wider audience, we chose to focus on the personalities that created these policies. Human stories are always universally interesting, but writing about South Korean politicians is a daunting task. We have tried to be objective with the contribution of each Mayor. We focused on assessing only the work they did during their time in office because this book is not a political work. We also tried not to make any commentary about the totality of their lives and careers but simply to take a look at what brought them to the mayor's office and what smart city policies they implemented. While we do assert that most of what we cover in this book is visionary, any perception that we are favoring one political party over another is unintended.

Because the objective of this book is to make the Korean experience digestible for international audiences, we have also sought to write an English-language book with clear Korean influences. For this reason, we have written Korean names with the surname first, for instance, not 'Myung-bak Lee' but 'Lee Myung-bak.' It is normal in Korea for people to present themselves with their surname first, so we have opted to stay true to that practice instead of adapting to the western practice of stating one's given name first. In addition, we have included the **Hangul**, the Korean alphabet, writing for most proper nouns like Seoul (서울) to help readers become familiar with Hangul and because it adds a uniquely Korean aesthetic quality to the text.

All in all, it is our sincere hope that this book helps people understand how Seoul has been transformed into a smarter and more sustainable city. As it is a city that we both love, it is likely that we have been unable to neutralize our attachment to it. But we think that this is also part of the story. As both citizens (like Dr. Park) and visitors (like myself) began to feel more confident in the way they interacted with Seoul, the more invested they became in its success. Just as locals were empowered to start a business to enhance the vibrancy of the city or just as Koreaphiles from around the world start businesses to raise the profile of South Korea, the intention of this writing is to shine a light on the development of smart city services in Seoul in an effort to inspire other cities to follow Seoul's example.

Kristi Shalla
September 2023

Introduction

South Korea emerged in the late 2010s as the capital of Asian cool. In the ten years preceding the publishing of this book, Korean culture has become a unique and powerful global phenomenon extending its reach to the most extreme and isolated parts on the planet. No Asian country has had this kind of diverse level of success in the Western world, not even Japan with the boom of manga culture in the 1990s. The pop group BTS has changed the way the world sees East Asian culture and has helped to shatter the 'model minority myth' in Western countries. Artists like Bong Joon-Ho (groundbreaking director of the film *Parasite*), Lee Jung-Jae (actor from the Netflix series *Squid Game*), Youn Yuh-Jung (actor from the film *Minari*), and Psy (the singer of the hit song *Gangnam Style*) have given definitions to the uniqueness of Korean culture in both the Asian and global contexts. And international beauty standards have been altered and made more diverse by the rise of the Korean beauty industry. In the early 2020s, it seems like everyone wants to take a dip in the **Korean wave**.

But South Korea was not always a global reference for **soft power**. As recently as the year 2000, South Korea was relatively unknown on the world stage and few people outside of East Asia had any sense of Korean culture. This change in perception wasn't luck; it was the product of a series of strong and deliberate policy decisions by the government and hard work on the part of the private sector and the general population.

This book aims to examine the way in which South Korea has been transformed from a developing nation to one of the world's largest economies through the process of urban development in the capital city of Seoul. The rise of Korean culture is a direct result of the shift by the Korean government to focus on sustainable development after joining the Organization for Economic Cooperation and Development (OECD) in 1996. There are many lessons from the Korean experience that can help other cities around the globe to build a smarter and more sustainable environment in which their citizens can flourish.

In the early 2000s, Seoul was a less attractive city than it is today. Despite being a successful economic, political, and financial hub, the city faced serious challenges that were common among fast-growing cities at the time. The population density in Seoul was on par with that of other mega-cities in developing nations, such as Jakarta, Mexico City, and Rio de Janeiro. From 1953 to 1988, Seoul's population increased tenfold from about 1 million to 10 million. In 2000, 20% of the Korean population lived in the city, and the percentage rose to nearly 50% when considering the *Seoul Capital Area*, which includes the metropolitan areas of Incheon and Gyeonggi province. These numbers put a strain on the city's resources and infrastructure, leading to issues such as housing and transportation shortages, traffic jams, air pollution, and overuse of resources. The streets were often crowded with cars, and the air was often filled with smog. Additionally, residents were faced with unpleasant conditions, such as dirty and overcrowded streets.

Seoul's transformation over the past two decades has been nothing short of remarkable, thanks in large part to the efforts of three mayors: Lee Myung-bak (2002–2006), Oh Se-hoon (2006–2011, 2021–), and Park Won-soon (2011–2020). These leaders have used technology, data, and sustainability planning to reshape the urban experience in South Korea's capital and set the stage for continued growth and development. It is worth noting that these three mayors came from different political parties and had distinct visions for the city, yet all understood the power of technology and data to bring about citizen-centered changes. Their work serves as a valuable example for other cities in the midst of rapid development, as it followed a period of rapid growth and demonstrated how smart city policies can ease the transition to becoming a global economic hub with a high quality of life.

Lee Myung-bak   **Oh Se-hoon**   **Park Won-soon**

(Source: Wikipedia Commons)

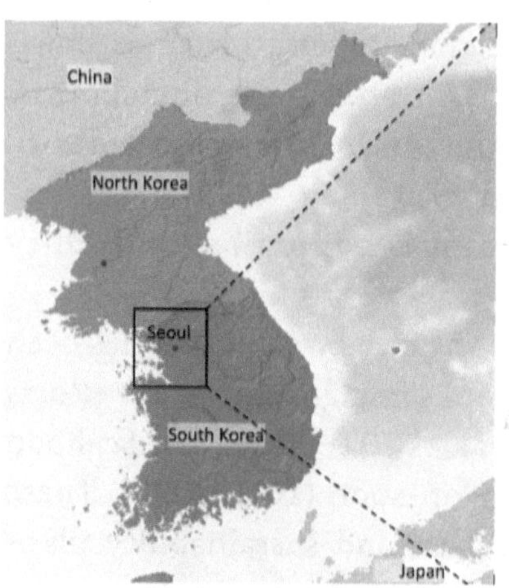

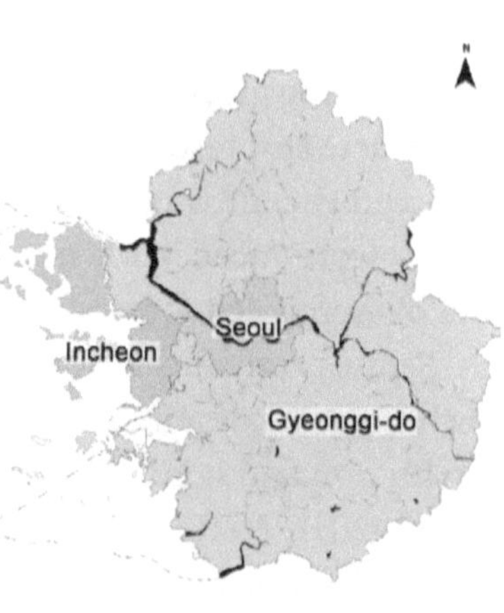

**Location of Seoul in South Korea (Left) and
Seoul's Capital Area (Right)**
(Source: Wikipedia Commons)

We will start with setting the scene for Seoul's smart city development story by reviewing how South Korea overcame the destruction of the Korean War and achieved the economic growth often termed *The Miracle on the Han River*[1]. We will also look specifically at how the city of Seoul rapidly transformed from a city in ruins to a sprawling megacity with new opportunities for residents but also a multitude of urban problems. After that, we will look chronologically at urban interventions implemented by each of the three mayors, and how these measures not only relieved the growth pains felt by city residents but also enabled a dynamic expansion of Korean soft power.

A term used frequently in this book is *smart city*. There is not a simple or straightforward definition of what a smart city is. The term smart city has become fashionable globally to describe digitally enhanced urban interventions. It is also interchanged with the terms 'sustainable city' or 'ubiquitous city,' usually when the term 'smart city' is politicized. Local governments in the United States have a preference for using the word 'sustainable' instead of 'smart' when talking about urban interventions using technology because they feel the word *smart* focuses too much on technology, and this is a political issue for a vocal portion of their constituency. Similarly, the *'Ubiquitous City'* or 'U-city' program took off in South Korea in the early 2000s and only relatively recently has the term smart city become commonplace when discussing urban interventions. This interchanging of non-equal terms across different geographic and language groups can often cause confusion but, in the end, it all means the same thing – *the improvement of the urban landscape through the use of technology and data*. This book uses the term 'smart city' as a broader term to include a wide range of urban interventions

---

[1] 'The Miracle of the Han River' is a term that symbolizes South Korea's fast post-war recovery and rapid economic growth in the 1970s and 1980s. This phrase came into common usage after South Korea came on the world scene by successfully hosting the 1988 Seoul Olympic Games.

to make cities more sustainable and citizen-friendly.

Smart cities are mainly composed of three features. First, technology and connectivity are essential tools for smart cities. Advanced technologies like *Big Data, Internet of Things (IoT), Artificial Intelligence (AI), 5G,* and many other innovative technologies are the basis of a smart city. Secondly, smart city development and implementation practices use technology to solve urban problems and improve the quality of life in cities. Ubiquitously deployed CCTVs across a city can prevent urban crimes and help to catch criminals. Smart parking solutions can ease traffic congestion and carbon emissions by guiding drivers directly to empty parking spots with less cruising time. IoT sensors can consistently monitor and ensure the quality of drinking water. Drones can deliver essential health supplies in remote or underserved cities. Third and most importantly, local or national governments use smart city projects as a means of driving economic growth and improving quality of life. Innovative content like *Virtual Reality (VR)* or *Augmented Reality (AR)* combined with local history and culture can attract more tourists. *Open Data* can contribute to attracting and fostering start-ups as well by allowing start-ups to experiment and launch new service models or products with less private investment.

As the advancement of smart city development depends heavily on the adoption of technology, Seoul is an ideal case study. Seoul is highly ranked in many global smart city surveys like the United Nations E-government Survey, Digital Cities Index from the Economist Impact, Smart Cities Ranking from Juniper's Research, etc. *Seoulites* in 2023 benefit from decades of smart city planning and economic development strategies to make their life more convenient and prosperous. The air in the city has become fresher, and the streets have gotten cleaner. More pleasant cycling, walking, or resting spaces have popped up across the city. Citizens' access to civic services or social welfare benefits has increased.

Although Seoul is far from perfect, our hope is that Seoul's transformation over the past 20 years can serve as inspiration for other cities around the world for developing a more sustainable and citizen-oriented urban experience. Throughout this book, we attempt to illustrate six essential ideas related to smart city building that have enabled such a successful transformation of the urban environment in Seoul and that can serve as practical advice for city officials around the globe:

1. *Local autonomy serves as the cornerstone of smart city development. In South Korea, a pivotal moment for Korean cities came in 1995 with the introduction of direct elections for local government leaders. This shift empowered local officials to create solutions to local problems.*

2. *Financial capability is the catalyst for transforming cities into smarter, more sustainable models. Smart services are enabled by costly cutting-edge technologies and become feasible for implementation only when a city's physical infrastructure requirements are met and the city has financial flexibility.*

3. *Effective leadership is the key to the successful implementation of smart and sustainable technologies. Many smart city interventions may be unpopular at first, costly, or take longer than expected to be appreciated, so clear and collaborative city leadership is essential to lead smart city projects to completion.*

4. *A holistic approach is imperative. Although some interventions might seem very localized, smart city interventions often require interfacing between different technologies and collaboration between multiple organizational units. The city government needs to consider how each intervention will affect the entirety of the urban community.*

5. *Community engagement is a powerful and effective tool for urban innovation. Although visionary government leadership plays a pivotal role in facilitating the transition to a smart city, technology is advancing faster than many politicians can keep up with. The private sector, academia, and city residents can offer valuable contributions in the form of knowledge, cutting-edge technologies, and innovative ideas, serving as indispensable partners in the development and execution of smart initiatives tailored to the local community's needs.*

6. *The IT industry ecosystem is an essential partner in the implementation of smart city services. Without a robust cluster of IT companies capable of proposing and implementing cutting-edge smart services, realizing the vision of a smart city can be challenging, potentially resulting in undesirable outcomes such as heavy reliance on global IT giants and national security concerns.*

Each urban space is different and has its own challenges and advantages. This book is a case study of a relatively common scenario of a fast-growing economy looking to establish itself among the world's most developed nations. Some cities are unable to get over this hurdle of chaotic development and it inhibits their ability to make that final push into becoming a first world nation and global influencer. The government of Seoul and South Korea have been incredibly successful in harnessing the chaos that existed at the end of the high-growth cycle and channeling it into sophisticated development. The making of modern Seoul is relevant to cities around the world. To glean valuable lessons from Seoul's experience, we must first understand the conditions in South Korea and the city of Seoul that enabled the development of the city as a leading smart city.

FROM RUINS TO
MEGA-CITY

Chapter 1
Export-led Growth and Democracy Building

The region we know as the *Korean Peninsula* (한반도)[2] was independent through most of human civilization and boasts over 5,000 years of recorded history. At a time when the world was in chaos due to World War I (1914–1918) and World War II (1939–1945), the Korean Peninsula was under Japanese control after the Empire of Japan annexed Korea in 1910. Japan sought to incorporate Korean territory into Japan by suppressing Korean culture and identity. The independence movement to fight the Japanese occupation led to diverging ideologies[3] of the leaders of the post-war Korean government, and soon after gaining independence from Japan at the end of WWII, a civil war later referred to as 'The Korean War' broke out in June 1950. The war ended three years later with the division of the Korean Peninsula into two nations along the 38th parallel[4]: the Republic of Korea (South Korea) and the Democratic People's Republic of Korea (North Korea).

The modern era of South Korea started in the early 1950s

---

[2] The Korean Peninsula is over 900 km long and bordered by China and Russia to the north. Refer to the Figure on page 10.

[3] South Korea allied with the United States for the development of a free-market democracy and North Korea allied with the Soviet Union for the development of a centrally-planned, communist state.

[4] The name given to latitude 38° N. The 38th parallel roughly demarcates the border between North Korea and South Korea on the Korean peninsula.

**Korean Women and Childeren Searching for
Firewood in War Ruins**
(Source: US Army official Korean War Image Archive)

after the Korean War left the entire peninsula in ruins. At the end of WWII, South Korea was put under a US Protectorate until Rhee Syng-man (이승만), a Korean who had lived most of his adult life in the United States, was elected in 1948 in a democratic election supervised by US armed forces. Rhee Syng-man ruled the country for 12 years from 1948 to 1960,[5] with the goal of strengthening democracy and capitalism in the post-war rebuilding phase. After years of economic stagnation and weak democratic development, a student protest movement called the April Revolution (4.19 혁명) ousted Rhee. A brief transitional government was set up before army general Park Chung-hee (박정희) seized power on May 16, 1961, in a May 16 Coup d'Etat[6] (5.16 군사정변).' After taking office,

---

[5] He was re-elected as the president two more times and fraudulent voting took place in his fourth presidential election.

[6] The military coup took advantage of the temporary moment of anarchy caused by the April Revolution. Although it was launched due to

Park Chung-hee spent the rest of the decade solidifying his power under an authoritarian military regime and preparing South Korea for economic expansion.

Rhee Syng-man
(Source: Seoul Museum of History)

Park Chung-hee
(Source: Wikipedia Commons)

Park Chung-hee ruled for 18 years as the president of South Korea until Kim Jae-gyu (김재규), the director of the Korean Central Intelligence Agency (KCIA), assassinated him on October 26, 1979. South Korea's economy experienced remarkable growth during his term (1961–1979), even though he became increasingly authoritarian after 1972 with the implementation of the Yushin Order (유신체재). As the popularity of politician Kim Dae-jung (김대중)[7] increased, Park Chung-hee felt a threat to perpetuating his presidency and, in the end, dissolved the National Assembly and suspended the Constitution under the Yushin Order. The Yushin Order

dissatisfaction with the government, there was not a clear administrative plan in place at the time of the coup d'etat.

[7] Kim Dae-jung, may be globally known as DJ, is a figure called the father of Korean democracy. He was heavily suppressed during the military regime because of his popularity. However, he eventually became the eighth president of South Korea from 1998 to 2003 and received the 2000 Nobel Peace Prize for his work for democracy and human rights in South Korea and in East Asia. He is the only and first Korean to have won the Nobel Prize to date.

lasted until 1979 and this period is sometimes referred to as the era of **developmental dictatorship** (개발독재). This era was pivotal to the country's development because it was characterized by a period of high economic growth paired with a culture of protest and repression. Many of the modern leaders of South Korea were involved in protests against the Yushin Order as students, and this era shaped the focus on the egalitarian local policy that we see in South Korea today.

Like his peers of the 20th century, Mustafa Atatürk of Turkey, Lee Kuan Yew of Singapore, and Deng Xiaoping of China, Park Chung-hee used centralized, authoritarian leadership to rebuild South Korea, although Park did so with less previous experience in government than the other three. Park Chung-hee put the economy first. He devised successive five-year economic and social development plans, allocated resources for these plans and pushed industry and society hard to meet growth targets. He built major highways, industrial complexes, nationwide multi-purpose dams and promoted export-led growth strategies. As a result, South Korea's Gross Domestic Product (GDP) per capita grew from $94 in 1961 to over $1000 in 1977, and exports surpassed $1 billion in 1970, multiplying tenfold from 1964. Rural areas were transformed through a policy called 'Saemaul Undong[8] (새마을운동),' which many developing countries still use as a benchmark today as best practice in rural development initiatives. President Park's measures, although authoritarian and questioned by human rights activists, were effective in producing an average growth rate in the 1970s of over 10.5%.

After the assassination of President Park Chung-hee in late 1979, the authoritarian military regime continued for another

---

[8.] South Korea's self-help new village movement initiative launched in 1970. The government provided resources like sacks of cement and villagers modernized their houses and rural infrastructure such as roads. The movement also encouraged villagers to carry out income-generating projects like pig farming and off-season vegetable cultivation.

eight years under his successor, Chun Doo-hwan (전두환). The administration of Chun Doo-hwan was responsible for the violent suppression of the Gwangju Uprising (5.18 광주민주화운동), which led to the tragic death of hundreds of pro-democracy activists by the military forces in 1980. This event had a profound effect on the Korean psyche and ushered in an era of elevated political consciousness, including the proliferation of socio-political arts such as the Minjung art[9] (민중미술) movement as well as literary and cinematic works. Most of the early 1980s were spent in political disarray with pro-democracy protests on a massive scale across the country. Eventually, the military regime ended with the 1987 June Democracy Movement (6.10 민주항쟁), a nationwide pro-democracy protest, which lasted for 20 days from June 10 to June 29 and was depicted in the 2017 Korean blockbuster film *1987: When the Day Comes*. After the June Democracy Movement, the administration of Chun Doo-hwan could no longer keep democracy at bay and agreed to a democratic presidential election, promising a peaceful transition of power. The administration also agreed to the development of local autonomy systems for the democratic election of local government officials[10]. These local democratic systems were implemented in the 1990s, and the first local election to elect governors, metropolitan and municipal mayors, and local legislatures took place in 1995. The revival of local autonomy systems in South Korea was the first step toward a transparent, people-oriented government and the transformation of Korean cities.

---

[9] Minjung art originates from the artwork produced for and used in protests. This Art movement was born with the democratization movement against the military regime in South Korea and continued under the post-military government for a while. As South Korea developed a stronger democracy, Minjung art has shifted to exploring various social themes such as labor and minority rights and mass culture.

[10] Local elections were abolished by Park's military coup in favor of the assignment of local governors by central government to ensure direct control at local levels.

Even in this turbulent period, economic growth in South Korea remained high. The government of Chun Doo-hwan started off under gloomy economic conditions when he took power in 1980. South Korea's economy took a downturn in the late 1970s, with the GDP growth rate contracting by -1.6%, while inflation jumped to 28.7%. For this reason, Chun Doo-hwan focused more on price stabilization than economic growth and took a different approach to fostering industries. President Park had encouraged heavy industries with conglomerates such as Hyundai and Daewoo, but Chun Doo-hwan favored *Information Technology (IT)* and the electronics industry. Under Chun's stabilization policies, IT companies such as Samsung and LG were able to invest in long-term goals to modernize their product lines and their organizational structure. As a result, the inflation rate stabilized at 2.3% in 1984, and economic growth rebounded to 13.4% in 1983. He also prioritized promoting South Korea on the world stage by hosting the 1986 Asian and 1988 Olympic Games.

The 1990s proved a pivotal decade in the preparation of South Korea as a global center of sustainable development. As presidents with no military ties were elected by direct universal suffrage, the economic and political systems of South Korea evolved into a form of western-style capitalism (e.g., separation of business and government) and democracy (e.g., citizen empowerment). This set the scene for the rollout of sustainability policy in the 2000s.

Because the previous decades had successfully overcome the administrative hurdles of capacity building and democracy building, the new decade saw many of these democratic and industrial high-achievers enter the political arena to guide Korea's development to the next level. Furthermore, South Korea was still riding the wave of high economic growth, which incorporated higher levels of technology and modernization into its corporate structure. It was in the 1990s that companies like Samsung and LG turned the corner in efficiency and process to enable their global expansion in the early 2000s. With the economic growth of the 1960s and 1970s from Park Chung-hee's push for dynamic development and the subsequent years of democratic and industrial reforms in both the public and private sectors, South Korea continued on the track of high-impact and sophisticated growth during the 1990s. Neither the 1997 IMF crisis[11] nor the late 1990s global dot-com crash[12] could thwart South Korea's socio-economic rise. Overall growth in South Korea in the 1990s averaged over 8%, but what is truly significant is that after the economy contracted heavily at -5.13% in 1998, it rebounded at lightning speed to grow at 11.47% in 1999.

The 1990s was also a pivotal decade in South Korea for structural change. In 1996, South Korea joined the OECD as a full member. The OECD's focus on data-driven policymaking and sustainable development brought about a new sense of consciousness about South Korea's place in the global economy and formed the basis for the rise of smart city policy in the 2000s.

"Joining the OECD meant transforming from a developing country to a developed country," described former Ambassador to the United States Choi Seok-young (최석영). "It wasn't simple. The OECD officials were surprised that there was a gap between the laws in force and their actual enforcement, so we had to focus on closing that gap. OECD membership also made us focus on environmental policy and labor rights."

With economic, political and structural reform taking place in rapid succession over the last three decades of the 20th

---

[11] A financial crisis experienced by Korean people. The Korean government requested a rescue package from the International Monetary Fund (IMF). In return, Korean companies had to conform to internationally accepted accounting and auditing standards following IMF supervision.

[12] A stock market bubble caused by speculation in dotcom or internet-based businesses from 1995 to 2000. In 2000, the dot-com bubble burst, and many dot-com startups went out of business after burning through their venture capital and failing to become profitable.

century, South Korea was poised to make the leap to become a global leader. Nowhere were the events of South Korea's modern history of growth and reform felt more strongly than in the capital city of Seoul, and nowhere was the economic miracle so clearly transformed into smart and sustainable growth in the first twenty years of the 21st century.

Chapter 2

The Rise of Seoul as a Global Economic Power

As Korea's economic and political center, Seoul plays an over-sized role in representing South Korea abroad. It is the world's 6th wealthiest metropolitan area after Tokyo, New York, Los Angeles, London, and Paris. The GDP of Seoul in 2021 was nearly $927 billion, larger than that of the Netherlands or Mexico. Over 75% of South Korea's 100 largest companies, like LG and Hyundai, are headquartered in Seoul. Seoul is also the political capital where both South Korea's presidential office and the national assembly are located. As of 2022, about 10 million people, 20% of the total population of South Korea, live in Seoul. Just as many people from all over the world flock to the United States with the American dream, young Koreans flock to Seoul hoping to obtain high-paying jobs and a sophisticated lifestyle. Seoulites have become admired throughout Asia and the world for their style as representatives of the Korean Wave soft power movement.

Seoul's position as the capital city traces back to 1392 when Joseon, Korea's last dynasty (1392–1910), was founded. At that time, Joseon ruled most of the Korean Peninsula and established *Hanyang* (the name was later changed to Seoul) as the capital city in 1394 because of its strategic location in the center of the territory. Since then, Seoul has served as the capital for more than 600 years, and this is the reason why cultural heritage sites like traditional palaces can be found among modern and high-tech buildings in the center of the city today.

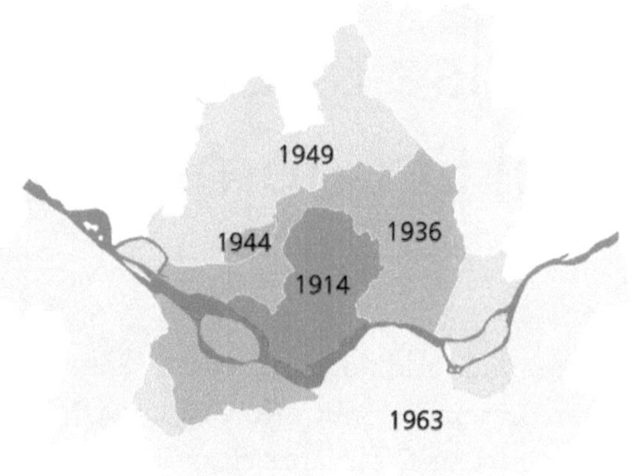

Territorial History of Seoul (1914–1995)

The area of Seoul covers 605 km^2, similar to the size of Tokyo, Japan (644 km^2). In the Joseon era, the total area of Seoul was much smaller at 16.5 km^2. The area of Seoul has grown substantially over the centuries, with massive expansions during both the Japanese colonial regime and the military dictatorship. During the Japanese colonial period (1910–1945), the Japanese government considered Seoul a forward base for Japan's advance into China and developed Seoul as an industrial and transportation center. The land area of Seoul was expanded during this period as its corresponding development of residential and industrial districts increased. The largest expansion of Seoul's land area, especially the area south of the Han River, took place during Park Chung-hee's regime, partially as a defensive strategy to guard against a possible attack from the North. At the outbreak of the Korean War, Seoul had fallen in only four days, so Park felt that if the city was developed on both sides of the river, the south side would have a better chance of resisting because of the natural water barrier and the government could be evacuated south.

In the expansion process, Seoul developed three distinctive elements: *the Han River* (한강), *Gangbuk* (강북) and *Gangnam* (강남). The Han River is the most important part of the city of Seoul and the lifeblood of the urban community. It is a water resource for 10 million Seoulites. The total length of the Han River is about 494 km, of which 41.5 km is included in the administrative district of Seoul. It is a kilometer-wide river that flows through Seoul and divides the city into two regions: Gangnam and Gangbuk. Twenty-two bridges have been built over the Han River to connect the north and south sides of the city. The riversides of the Han River provide environmentally-friendly recreation spaces such as pedestrian walkways, bike paths, and public squares. The Han River also offers visitors and residents spectacular night views of Seoul with several illuminated bridges.

The second is the area of the city north of the river called Gangbuk. Gangbuk is the historical center of Seoul, where the central business district, most government buildings and historical sites are located. Most of Seoul's signature tourist attractions and landmarks like Seoul Namsan Tower (남산타워), Gyeongbokgung Palace(경복궁), Bucheon Hanok Village (북촌 한옥마을), and Cheongwadae (청와대), known as the Blue House in English, are located in the Gangbuk area.

The third area is Gangnam. It was the inspiration for PSY's song "Gangnam Style" that created a global sensation in 2012. Gangnam indicates the southern districts of Seoul. A large land portion of Gangnam was composed of planned towns and commercial areas built on sites created by land reclaimed from the Han River. Those planned new towns in Gangnam became a wealthy area of Seoul, similar to Beverly Hills in Los Angeles. Seoul's signature modern buildings, such as Asia's largest underground mall, Starfield Coex Mall, and the world's

6th tallest skyscraper, Lotte World Tower, are located in and near the area. And as PSY describes in his song about cultivating a sophisticated lifestyle, the wealthiest area in Gangnam is home to many high-end department stores, luxury stores, and up-scale restaurants.

As in many other cities, strategic urban planning played a central role in forming today's spatial structure of Seoul. It was in 1962 that the Korean government established the Urban Planning Act, and the Seoul government started to set up and implement urban master plans and development projects after 1966[13]. In particular, the Tri-Center Urban Development Plan greatly shaped Seoul's multi-centric spatial structure of today. Until the early 1970s, Seoul had only a single city center located in Gangbuk. As the city modernized, the area around this center was becoming overcrowded and the number of informal dwellings skyrocketed. The Seoul administration sought to balance development through urban planning by distributing Seoul's city functions into centers in different geographical areas of the city. Through the Tri-Center Urban Development Plan, the city structure reform took place, and it created the industrial center in the southwest area of the Han River (Yeouido and Yeongdeungpo, 여의도와 영등포) and the financial center in the southeast region (Yeongdong and Jamsil, 영동과 잠실). The Plan was effective in decentralizing Seoul's population and city functions, and reducing a multitude of problems related to overcrowding and equitable development.

Meanwhile, several redevelopment projects have transformed

---

[13] Once, the Seoul administration proposed a full-scale master plan proposal called The New Seoul City Plan, which envisioned building a new capital city from scratch. But the Korean government disapproved of the Plan, which required large-scale budget execution. The plan was proposed under President Park's military regime when the central government appointed local governors and mayors. At the time, it was common that budgets for urban planning prioritized national initiatives and provided no accountability to residents of Seoul.

the Han River from an element posing a potential threat to the city to essential city infrastructure and a leisure center for Seoul citizens. The Seoul administration reclaimed land from the river, limited the threat of flooding and built highways along the riverbanks to connect bridges with the city and Park's new national highway system. New town plans and high-rise apartment developments south of the river injected housing supply units into Seoul. In preparing for the 1986 Asian Games and the 1988 Olympic Games, issues related to quality of life in Seoul first came to the forefront of the Han River development. The Seoul government started to improve the overall water quality of the Han River and create sports playgrounds and waterfront parks for citizens on the riverside.

Even with the reforms in the 1980s, Seoul continued to grow at a chaotic pace. The revival of local elections in 1995 brought about a turning point in Seoul's development policy. The first Mayor of Seoul was Cho Soon (조순), South Korea's former finance minister (1988–1990) and central bank governor (1992–1993). The person who succeeded Cho Soon was Goh Kun (고건), the former Prime minister of South Korea (1997-1998), who would also serve as Prime Minister again after his term as Mayor. South Korea's administration system in the 1990s was centralized, and the responsibility to empower the roles and rights of local governments fell under elected provincial governors in the early days. Cho and Goh put a lot of effort into establishing South Korea's local autonomy system and made initial steps toward developing urban policies to improve the life of Seoul's growing population during their terms as Mayors of Seoul.

It was really in 2002 that local officials began to actively focus on solving local problems and initiated the transition from a growth-driven city to a sustainable smart city. With the election of Lee Myung-bak, the city started moving toward the development of smart city technology. The mayoral terms of Lee Myung-bak (2002–2006), Oh Se-Hoon (2006–2011,

2021–), and Park Won-Soon (2011–2020) were key to the transformation of South Korea's capital city from an overcrowded megacity spiraling out of control to a resilient city included in the list of top 20 livable cities globally[14]. All three mayors were controversial figures in Korean politics, and we will not examine the totality of their political life. Rather, we will look to examine their advances in urban development and how they not only implemented effective smart city policies but also how they developed plans for these policies.

The Miracle on the Han River has given the world a lesson in high-growth policy-making for countries in development, but what is equally worth examining is how this dense, middle-income metropolis of the early 2000s was able to transform into a global reference for smarter and sustainable city building during the time it was also undergoing dynamic population and income growth.

This work is meant to serve as a guide on how Seoul was transformed from an Asian mega-city with all of the trappings of decades of high growth and runaway population density into a smart and sustainable city. We will look at policy and reform with the objective of showing other cities what steps were taken to transform the public and private sectors as well as citizen engagement to bring about changes in economic development and growth.

---

[14] Monocle magazine ranked Seoul number 11 in their 2021 list of 'Most livable cities,' ahead of all North American cities on the list.

PART II

BUILDING A SUSTAINABLE CITY

Chapter 3
The Bulldozer Takes Seoul

Lee Myung-bak (이명박) is one of the most famous mayors in the world when it comes to sustainable city development. Nicknamed "Bulldozer" during his career in the private sector, he had an exceptional ability to find high-impact projects and push them to rapid completion. Few single local government administrations have laid so much groundwork for sustainable development in a dense, urban setting, and his signature projects have become classic case studies in the greening of urban spaces and transport reform for city planners around the world. His recognizable achievements on sustainable development led him to become the 17th president of Korea (2008–2013) after his term as Seoul's 3rd democratically-elected mayor (2002–2006) and gave him the opportunity to extend his vision on sustainable development to the national level.

Lee Myung-bak's biography reads like a Korean period drama. He was born in 1941 in Osaka, Japan, during World War II. Korea had been occupied by Japan since 1910, and his family had moved to Osaka so his father could work as a farmhand. When the war ended and Japan was left in ruins, his family returned to Korea in a makeshift boat that capsized halfway across the Korea Strait. They arrived in his father's hometown of Pohang (포항), located on the eastern coastline of South Korea, with only their clothes on their backs. The family was desperately poor, and Lee Myung-bak has often recounted that it was not unusual for him to go to bed hungry. To make things worse, the Korean War broke out soon after their return, and Lee Myung-bak witnessed the death of two of his siblings during this conflict.

Raised by a Christian mother, Lee Myung-bak was taught the value of work and the list of odd jobs he did to help his family put food on the table is endless: he sold rice cakes, homemade matches, popcorn in front of an all-girls school, and about anything he could get his hands on. He was an excellent student and took classes in the evening at a commercial high school (similar to the vocational high schools we know today) on a full scholarship. Upon completion of high school, he was admitted to Korea University (고려대학교)[15] in Seoul and started studies in Business Administration in 1961. Not only a brilliant student, Lee Myeong-bak was also popular with his classmates and became student council president in 1964. Later that year he joined protests against Korean-Japan negotiations, an effort by Park Chung-hee's government toward the normalization of the diplomatic relations between Korea and Japan after the Japanese colonial occupation of Korea. He was arrested and jailed for his participation and spent three months in Seodaemun Prison (서대문형무소)[16].

Upon release, Lee Myung-bak completed his studies and joined Hyundai Construction (현대건설) in 1965. He was a star at Hyundai and quickly rose in the ranks to become a company director at age 29. At the age of 35, he was appointed the Chief Executive Officer of Hyundai Construction Corporation, the predecessor of today's Hyundai Group, which is South Korea's second-largest conglomerate. This meteoric rise was

---

[15] Korea University is one of the three most prestigious institutions of higher learning in South Korea.

[16] Korea's first modern prison facility. This prison was opened in 1908 by the Japanese Administration to imprison pro-independence activists and closed in 1987. The place was remodeled as a prison history museum and opened to the public. The museum is still open today.

exceptional during the Park Chung-Hee years in South Korea. Although growth rates were high in South Korea during the 1960s and 70s, it was unusual for someone without family connections or political support to rise so far so fast. At age 47, he was promoted to the head of Hyundai Group (현대그룹). In the late 1980s, he became well known in Korea as a successful businessman.

It surprised Korean people greatly when he decided to leave the private sector to enter politics in 1992, at age 51. In retrospect, there had been a perception among Koreans that politics and economics were two different worlds. Few people thought that a highly successful businessperson like Lee Myung-bak, who had already acquired wealth and fame, would enter the political arena, but he felt he could contribute to the building of a better nation. With the nickname "Bulldozer" from his career at Hyundai, Lee Myung-bak was part of the wave of non-military leaders who set out to bring about change in South Korea by running for and winning the seat as the representative for Seoul's Jongno-gu[17] district to the national assembly.

Lee Myung-bak was an active member of the national assembly and his political power and popularity gradually increased and he won the race for Mayor of Seoul in 2002. Because of the prominent position the city of Seoul plays in the Korean political and economic landscape, the Mayor of Seoul is considered to be the second-highest profile political post in the country and a natural candidate for the presidency. After only ten years in politics, Lee Myung-bak used his unique mixture of dynamism and drive to rise as a political star in the same way he rose as a student leader at University and then as a high-flier in business.

Before being elected Mayor, he spent a year as a visiting

[17.] There are two common paths to becoming President in South Korea. One is to become the Mayor of Seoul and the other is to first be a congressman representing Jongno-gu.

scholar at George Washington University in Washington, DC. His experience in the United States changed his perspective toward urban development from purely a driver of economic growth to a platform for sustainable and human-centered economic development. During this time, he studied public works projects and was especially impressed by *The Big Dig Project* in Boston, Massachusetts. The Big Dig Project was a mega road infrastructure project that demolished an elevated highway in Boston and rerouted traffic to a 3.5-mile subterranean tunnel. This was done to remove the bulky cement overpasses meant for vehicular traffic from view and make way for greenspaces and sustainable transport options in the city of Boston.

The case would serve as inspiration for his signature project as Mayor of Seoul. His election platform included promises to improve the lives of all citizens and to transform Seoul into a sustainable city through a number of initiatives, including the restoration of the Cheonggyecheon (청계천) and the restructuring of the inefficient and crumbling transport system. In the end, he made good on these promises, even though he had to use his bulldozer tactics to get some things done. His success as mayor was based on a quick-win, private-sector mentality that earned him international accolades and paved the way for his presidential victory a few years later.

Lee Myung-bak has been a controversial figure in Korean politics since the 1990s, but his years as the Mayor of Seoul were unquestionably important as a turning point in creating a more livable city and key to earning Seoul global attention as the sustainable city we know today. In the next two chapters, we will examine Lee Myung-bak's two signature projects that put Seoul on the map as a global reference for urban redevelopment: the Seoul Public Transportation Reform (2002–2004) and the Cheonggyecheon Restoration Project (2003–2005).

Chapter 4

Putting People at the Center of Transport Policy

Winston Churchill once said, "*Victory is the beautiful, bright-colored flower. Transport is the stem without which it could never have blossomed.*" He understood how essential transportation is in daily life. It is the backbone of a city that allows it to function in an organized way and the means by which people access opportunities in life. When transport does not work properly, it can wreak havoc on the economic system in the city as well as the quality of life and health of residents.

Before the arrival of Lee Myung-bak as Mayor, Seoul was at an inflection point in traffic management. In the early 2000s, the use of private vehicles had increased substantially. Commuting time in Seoul was one of the highest in the world at around 92 minutes on average as the number of vehicles in the city rose to about 2.5 million and traffic density increased. Similar to the images of large cities around the world at the time, highways in Seoul had turned into "parking lots" during rush hour, with slow-moving traffic extending commute times and diminishing the welfare of commuters. Meanwhile, bus ridership in Seoul was declining. Although the bus was traditionally the main mode of transportation in Seoul, service levels had become unreliable, forcing Seoulites to look for other, often more expensive, transport options. In Winston Churchill's terms, transportation in the city of Seoul was hampering the blossoming of economic activity.

With this in mind, Lee Myung-bak decided to carry out the biggest transportation reform in the history of South Korea. He knew that in order for Seoul to reach the next level of growth and prosperity, the city needed to be more organized and hospitable. As part of his campaign promise to improve the lives of the people of Seoul, Lee Myung-Bak advocated for an overhaul of the public transport system and his goal of turning downtown Seoul into a human-oriented space.

Seoul had grown dynamically during the postwar years, and with this growth came a myriad of transport issues. Even though the number of buses in Seoul increased rapidly from 230 units in 1953 to over 2,000 units in 1962, there was still an overcrowding problem. To solve Seoul's chronic bus shortage in the late 1960s, the city government had no choice but to allow bus operators to increase the number of buses without limit. With so many more vehicles on the road, traffic congestion began to skyrocket, and additional roads had to be built. The road network in Seoul nearly quadrupled between 1965 and 1970 from 1,440 km to 5,292 km to keep up with the city's expansion.

In 1971, the government ushered in a new phase of multi-modal transport in the city with the construction of the city's first metro line, an effort to improve overall mobility in the city and relieve some of the stress on the road network. Seoul Subway Line 1 started operations on August 15, 1974, and transported 31.77 million passengers in its first 4.5 months of operation. Although it was extremely successful, the subway quickly exceeded its transport capacity to the extent that it was nicknamed 'hell subway,' and buses remained an important form of transport for the people of Seoul. Around this time, the Korean automobile industry was also starting to take off. Kia's first passenger vehicle, the Brisa (브리사), was introduced in 1974, and Hyundai Motors also launched the Pony (포니) in 1975. This situation encouraged people to indulge in the newly affordable luxury of a private vehicle as an alternative to the overcrowded and unreliable public transportation system in Seoul. The influx of car traffic on roads only exacerbated the congestion problem as this less-dense form of individual transport started crowding roads and making bus services even slower and more unreliable.

The transportation landscape in the 1990s entered into a transition stage in the wrong direction. By the mid-1990s, Seoul was decades into a phase of rapid expansion that created massive urban sprawl and a steep increase in commuting times for residents. The transportation share of buses, close to 81.6% in the 1970s, fell to 28.8% at the end of the 1990s with the expansion of the metro system, which became the main form of transportation for the people of Seoul. After Seoul Subway Line 2 (the circular line serving both Gangnam and Gangbuk) opened in 1984, a few more lines were added and, by the late 1990s, the metro system's transportation share exceeded 35%. Automobiles were also catching up to buses as a preferred form of transportation in the city. The number of cars circulating in Seoul in 1990 had grown by a multiple of 50 since 1970, and the transportation share of cars was approaching 20%.

There were several reasons why bus ridership suffered such a steep decline. Even though buses were still the most accessible mode of transportation in the city, bus operations had become unreliable for many riders. The buses were not punctual, often canceled without notice, and there was little coordination between the various transport operators around the city. When the buses were running, they often skipped stops, and the bus drivers made riders uncomfortable by speeding and reckless driving. Seoul's public transportation system was extremely fragmented and lacked general oversight from city officials. City buses were run as private, for-profit businesses, and a variety of different operators had run services with separate payment methods in the metropolitan area, which resulted in a lack of coordination of transport services. Because the main corridors of the city were the highest traffic areas, the profit-seeking bus services competed with the new metro lines instead of complementing them and, as a result, many bus companies were increasingly losing customers to the metro system.

Many bus operators went out of business. By the year 2000, the number of buses in circulation had decreased to 8,000, down from over 10,000 in the 1970s. The number of bus operators also decreased from 103 in the mid-1990s to 58 in 2002. This situation resulted in a degradation of the quality of bus services. The lack of a coordinated transport plan for the city made the system chaotic, and the inconsistent and unreliable public transportation options compounded the congestion problem by pushing more people to private transportation options.

During the second half of the 1990s, a global movement focused on the greening of urban spaces started developing, and Lee Myung-bak was greatly influenced by the greenspaces in the United States during his stay in Washington, DC in the late 1990s. He campaigned on a platform of improving the quality of life in Seoul. After winning the Mayoral election in 2002, Lee Myung-bak made good on that promise by completely overhauling the public transport system to relieve the pain felt by commuters while moving toward the idea of a greener, more sustainable city center.

After a great deal of planning, Seoul's entire public transportation system was cut over to the new system on July 1, 2004. Bus routes, bus numbers, and fare payment methods changed overnight. As expected, the first day was close to mayhem and there was a massive amount of confusion for both riders and drivers. New fare terminals had been installed on city buses and many were not working properly, so there were a lot of complaints from passengers about miscalculated fares. Eventually, the kinks were worked out and the transportation system gradually stabilized over the first two weeks. Passengers began to adapt to the integrated fare system, and traffic congestion in downtown Seoul began to improve. The dedicated bus lanes increased the speed of public transit buses, and the absence of buses in the general traffic lanes improved the flow of private vehicle traffic on roads.

Roads in Seoul
(Source: Seoul Urban Solutions Agency)

Bus-only lanes give priority to buses on Seoul's roads and
separate them from the rest of road traffic with a dedicated lane
so that buses can run faster and more punctually.

Although the Seoul Public Transport Reform was launched in just one day, preparations for the reform took more than two years to plan and prepare. Mayor Lee Myung-bak believed that buses, as part of the transportation network in the city, should be a public service, and he often expressed this view when he addressed the public. He was so focused on this issue that he implemented a weekly transportation meeting in his schedule beginning the month he took office. As mayor of Seoul, he took a hands-on approach to understanding Seoul's current transportation issues and countermeasures and used his "bulldozer" tactics to ensure that the Seoul Public Transport Reform would positively impact the lives of the people of Seoul.

Mayor Lee Myung-bak's vision of the Seoul Public Transport Reform centered on the implementation of Bus Rapid Transit (BRT) lines and the integration of transport modes across the city. BRT is a reliable and fast bus service that features a dedicated lane and off-board fare collection so that it functions like a subway. It was created as an inexpensive and quick alternative to the long and infrastructure-heavy process of building a subterranean transport system. Curitiba, Brazil, launched one of the first BRT lines in 1974 and became a case study for BRT implementation globally. Lee Myung-bak visited Curitiba in 2003 to experience this system first-hand to better fit it into his transport reform plan.

The Seoul Public Transport Reform differed from the case of Curitiba in that Seoul was 4 times larger than Curitiba, and Curitiba had built an extensive BRT network *instead* of a subway system. In contrast, Seoul had a well-functioning subway system, so Lee Myung-bak looked at how the BRT could *complement* the existing subway system to move people more efficiently around the city.

The Seoul Public Transport Reform was a game changer, not only for South Korea but also as a global model for public transport efficiency. The scope of the reforms were wide-reaching, and the impact was dynamic. Seoul's public transport system was completely overhauled, adding distance-based fare systems, operator service-level-agreement based subsidies, and oversight for the whole system. This was done through three main mechanisms.

1. **Bus operators were given oversight and performance subsidies.**

   Before the Seoul Public Transportation Reform, the development of bus routes was left completely up to the bus companies, and most of the operators were poorly managed. This meant that a significant portion of mobility options in and around Seoul was left to private sector business people with little consideration for equitable transport. If the last two stops on each route were not profitable during certain hours of the day, these stops were simply not serviced. It also meant that decisions on route restructuring were based on profit and not equity, leaving those who most needed public transportation access without it.

Lee Myung-bak and his team did not want to fully privatize the bus system, but there were serious management issues that needed to be addressed. Besides the fact that their service was unreliable for users, 39 out of 58 bus operators were also losing money, and their annual deficit reached 22.8 billion KRW (about US$20 million). The solution was the implementation of a public-private partnership-based city-wide bus operation model called The Quasi-Public Bus System. The Seoul government took on a supervisory role in route development and network planning. The Seoul Transport Operation & Information Service (TOPIS) center was built for the comprehensive management of Seoul's public transport status and traffic data in the city. Bus operators maintained control over day-to-day operations and were given subsidies to improve their profitability, but service level agreements were put in place to ensure that service was reliable and consistent.

At first, the bus operators, and especially the bus drivers, disliked these new reforms and government oversight. Under the new system, fares were decreased to encourage transfers and service to less busy stops was mandated, so bus drivers worried this would cut into their income and protested this change. Gradually drivers came around because the city government expanded the number of bus routes in the city, effectively giving the drivers more job security, and took measures to minimize the dismissal of bus drivers. While the city government did not make bus operators public employees, they did structure salaries for bus drivers into their subsidies to operators, and they improved the bus drivers' welfare through measures such as guaranteed holidays and break times, support for school expenses for children, etc.

The Quasi-Public Bus System significantly contributed to transforming Seoul's bus service into a citizen-centered, equitable public service. Under the new system, bus operators could maintain bus routes that were not profitable without worrying about financial deficits. Since the bus network is the most agile form of transport in the city, the city government was able to use movement or location data of passengers or buses to regularly evaluate and improve the quality of bus service to reflect the changing transport patterns of the people of Seoul.

2. **Seoul's bus network was restructured to include a BRT line and color-coded bus types.**

It was significant not only that the bus network in Seoul was overhauled and coordinated, but also the way in which it was restructured. The new reforms organized the bus system in a very clear and efficient hub-and-spoke network, which enabled commuters to travel around the city with fewer transfers. The implementation of BRT lines also enabled express services for commuters who lived further from the city center. Starting with the 38.7 km of BRT lanes in 2004, the BRT system in Seoul has gradually expanded to 14 BRT routes covering

137 km. BRT stops were coordinated with subways and local buses throughout the city. Each type of bus was color-coded so that passengers could more easily differentiate between types of buses:

a. Blue – trunk line buses that connect areas outside of Seoul with downtown Seoul.

b. Green – branch line buses that run on shorter-distance routes and stop more frequently. They connect with most subway stations and bus stations.

c. Red – express buses that connect downtown Seoul with areas outside the city.

d. Yellow – circular line buses that run in a ring around the city center. They connect with blue line stops as well as major transport hubs and tourist destinations.

3. **All transport services in the city were consolidated into a unified smart card payment platform called 'T-Money.'**

City officials realized that to be effective, public transport should be coordinated and affordable. Reusable contactless payment cards were commonly used in large cities, including Seoul, at the time. Hong Kong had used Octopus Cards, which used a unified smart card payment system across a variety of operators (and even non-transport vendors). With the success of the Octopus Card, Lee Myung-bak saw an opportunity to build a more coordinated transport network in the city.

With the implementation of a smart card and the creation of an automated fare collection agency called the Korea Smart Card Company (KSCC), transport authorities in Seoul were able to unify payment for all public transportation into one platform and provide discounted pricing for transfers. This development allowed public transport users to transfer between transport modes and operators seamlessly and with the same payment method. This resulted in a higher level of ease for riders and enabled transport authorities to decrease overall fares to encourage public transportation use.

The overhaul of the public transport system in Seoul was a moonshot project for Lee Myung-bak. His goal was for the smart card to be used by 100% of transport users in Seoul. Before the reforms, usage of contactless payment cards was around 60%, but by 2014, after Lee Myung-bak had left office, smart card usage in Seoul rose to nearly 100% (98.9% of the population of Seoul used smart cards in 2014). This high penetration rate for smart card usage has had the added bonus of providing transport authorities with very precise and complete data on traveler behavior throughout the Seoul public transport system. Distance-based fare systems require riders to 'tag in' and 'tag out' of each transport carrier and mode. This means that transport authorities were able to see very clearly how people used the public transport system and were able to monitor how ridership changed as the number of riders increased, which has, in turn, also enabled authorities to expand the system with greater efficiency.

Lee Myung-bak and his team knew that they wanted to transform a functional city into a sustainable city, diminishing the growing pains associated with continued urban expansion. The Seoul Public Transport Reform was pivotal in creating a path to sustainable growth through providing a reliable and inexpensive alternative to private vehicles and decreasing levels of pollution and traffic congestion in the downtown Seoul area. These transport solutions also fomented the sense of community created by communal transport and changed the paradigm on what is considered a primary form of transport in the minds of the people of Seoul.

We will see in upcoming chapters how the Seoul government has continued to prioritize transport sustainability by making sure every new intervention in the transport network of the city is fully integrated with the smart card system and aligned with complementary transport options. In 2004, this level of user-friendly integration was revolutionary, and it changed the way both transport operators and city officials thought about the role of urban transport in the city to the extent that Seoul continues to be at the forefront of transport innovation 20 years later.

Key Takeaways:

- *Public transport is essential for the functioning of a city. A well-designed smart public transport system can improve the quality of life for residents and stimulate economic growth.*

- *Public transport reforms can be successful if they are comprehensive and well-planned. Strong leadership and government oversight are key to maintaining equity in public transportation.*

- *The Seoul Public Transport Reform is a model for other cities worldwide.*

Chapter 5

Bringing Nature into Downtown: Cheonggyecheon Restoration Project

The Cheonggyecheon (청계천) Restoration Project is arguably one of the most successful urban redevelopment projects of this century. This project brought nature back to the urban center by reviving a nearly 6-kilometer-long local stream that had been covered by a raised highway 50 years earlier. It was a project that virtually ushered in the age of sustainable city building, signaling the departure of the era of Korea as a developing economy and marking the current era of South Korea as a wealthy, developed economy. It is certainly one of the programs most emulated by other cities.

Cheonggyecheon was originally a natural stream that ran through Seoul for hundreds of years. The stream had been not only a source of drinking water for citizens but also an indispensable drainage system for the city where waste was dumped. By the beginning of the 20th century, Cheonggyecheon was quite dirty and polluted from overuse, like most urban waterways around the globe at the time. After World War II, the Cheonggyecheon area became the principal slum district in Seoul as war refugees and migrants from other parts of the country flocked to the area.

Rhee Syngman, South Korea's first president, implemented

plans to rebuild the capital city of Seoul into a modern city capable of accommodating the increased population. Part of his plan was to cover the Cheonggyecheon to eliminate the surrounding slum area, build more roads, and enable easier access to economic opportunities for citizens. This focus on the Cheonggyecheon area made it a central point for city planning, and as such, it played an important role in the development of Seoul during the following 40 years.

Under Park Chung-hee's presidency, the Cheonggye Elevated Motorway (청계고가도로) was built over the covered stream and opened in 1969. This overpass motorway signaled Korea's dedication to urban development and growth under the Western/US-led post-war model. It was used to separate slower inner-city traffic from high-speed intercity traffic passing through Seoul for Incheon, Korea's global logistics hub and port city. It enhanced the image of the area as the symbolic site of Seoul's rapid growth and modernization, and functionally took people off the streets by favoring the use of the private vehicle.

After 30 years of heavy use, the Cheonggye Motorway faced an unexpected fate. In the 1990s, two tragic accidents caused skepticism among Koreans toward development-led economic growth. The Seongsu Bridge disaster in 1994 and the Sampoong Department Store collapse in 1995 were disasters caused by fraudulent construction. The two incidents shocked the Korean people in the 1990s, much like the Itaewon tragedy of 2022. The Seongsu Bridge was a bridge over the Han River, and a section of the bridge collapsed into the river during the morning rush hour, killing 32 people. The Sampoong department store was a luxury store in one of Gangnam's new and central districts. Due to a structural failure, the building collapsed in a moment, killing 502 people.

During the economic boom of the 1960s and 70s, aggressive economic growth goals had fueled fast-paced development, which sometimes prioritized speed over quality. By the mid-1990s, some of the lower-quality construction was starting to show, and it created dangerous situations, such as these disasters that resulted in the deaths of innocent citizens. Meanwhile, the world was also beginning to pay attention to the need for sustainable development. Bringing green space back to the urban landscape could serve to ward off emerging environmental threats such as ozone layer destruction, global warming, and oil depletion. The Cheonggye Motorway started to emerge as a political issue as the need for repairs split opinion between those who thought it should be repaired and those who thought it should be removed.

Inspired by what he had seen in Boston a few years before, Lee Myung-bak advocated a removal and restoration plan. He reasoned that the highway was built to enable economic growth, which it had done well, but was impeding the creation of a better quality of life for Seoulites. His team correctly identified that the city was on the verge of growth in quality of the urban experience, and this meant beautification and sustainability.

The Cheonggyecheon Restoration Project was the cornerstone of Lee Myung-bak's 2002 mayoral campaign, and once in office, Lee's team set forth to put his plan into action. His leadership in carrying out this project would set a benchmark for the implementation of urban interventions globally.

Marion Weiss, an architect based in New York and the author of the book 'Deconstruction/Construction: The Cheonggyecheon Restoration Project in Seoul (2011)' points out the role of leadership and vision in this urban transformation.

"Indeed Mayor Myung-bak Lee chose the removal of the highway and the restoration of Cheonggyecheon as the central platform for his campaign in 2002. His commitment to improving the quality of life indices and restoring health to the city focused on the imperative of removing the highway and restoring the stream. While the transformation of stream to highway evolved from 1958 to 1977 within the objective criteria of transport design, Mayor Lee had the more complex obligation to establish and disseminate new terms and metrics defining an infinitely more subjective concept: quality of urban life. [...] Many political leaders have staked their legacies on urban transformations, but Lee Myung-bak set an unprecedented benchmark for speed and effectiveness, developing the proposal within months of his election and completing the project twenty-seven months after the beginning of the design process. With a diverse team of leaders from universities, business and ad hoc public groups, he effectively articulated the economic and cultural imperative to destroy the highway and restore the stream (p.48)."

To accomplish these goals, Mayor Lee Myung-bak set up three committees to develop and implement the project quickly. He knew that he needed this project to be completed within his first term as mayor because it was quite controversial and signaled a change in the way the people of Seoul would interact with their city. The three committees were to not only look after the implementation of the project but also the longer-term effects of the greater downtown development plans.

1. The Cheonggyecheon Restoration Headquarters oversaw the implementation of the restoration project. They were charged with making sure that the construction part of the process was on target, and the mayor met with them on a weekly basis to ensure that the project stayed on track.

2. The Cheonggyecheon Research Group was tasked with researching the effects of the removal of the highway and the creation of a human-oriented space. The group studied how the projects would affect transport, sanitation, the environment, culture and other urban indicators.

3. The Cheonggyecheon Citizens' Committee focused on citizen engagement and served as a public relations mechanism for Lee. Through this committee

the city government could collect public opinion and speak to the public about progress on implementation and how the project was improving the lives of citizens.

Cheonggyecheon in downtown Seoul
(Source: Seoul Metropolitan Government)

Wetland area in Cheonggyecheon
(Source: Seoul Metropolitan Government)

Cheonggyecheon at Christmas
(Source: Seoul Metropolitan Government)

The Cheonggyecheon Restoration Project was completed in 2005 and opened to the public on October 1st of the same year. It was a resounding success and attracted over 10 million visitors in the first 58 days. By the end of 2008, 75.5 million people had visited the space, an average of 64,000 people per day. The stream has revitalized this part of the city, with concerts and exhibitions happening year round and a return of foot traffic, as people who work in the area often take a break near the stream. The project has objectively transformed the downtown area of Seoul into a greener, more walkable, people-friendly space.

The Cheonggyecheon Restoration Project is also an early example of a nature-based solution in an urban setting. The project was originally criticized by environmentalists because of a significant amount of man-made intervention in the structural makeup of the renovated project and the fair amount of artificial maintenance required, but most of those critics quieted when they started to see the actual environmental effects of the project. Almost every type of ecological indicator exploded as life bloomed in the restored stream. Wildlife species increased from 98 to 626 in the first three years, including the return of plants, fish, insects and birds. The project also functioned as a cooling agent to reduce the heat-island effect in one of the most dense cities in the world. Estimates are that the existence of the Cheonggyecheon has brought about a decrease in maximum temperatures of 5 to 10% in the area.

Business in the area has also been transformed, with growth rates for new businesses double the average for other parts of downtown Seoul after the redevelopment and prices skyrocketing by 30 to 50% for properties within 50 meters of the restoration project, double the average increase in other areas of the city. Before the stream restoration project, the real estate values in the Gangbuk area were in decline. An increasing number of major companies had moved their headquarters from Gangbuk to Gangnam in the early 2000s. But since the opening of the Cheonggyecheon, the area has been revitalized and is once again competitive with Gangnam.

The effects of this project on the local economy came as no surprise. One of the principal reasons that Lee Myung-bak's administration prioritized this project was the increase in private sector investment to the surrounding neighborhood that they believed this project would bring about. The Cheonggyecheon Restoration Project was not just the beginning of a new era for South Korea, but it was also a project that introduced the idea that the city government could create a platform on which the private sector could thrive.

In a personal interview in 2014, Lee Myung-bak explained his motivation, "My thought was that Seoul should be not only a city where it is convenient for citizens to live in, but also a city that foreign investors could come and visit comfortably. There are various Asian cities like Shanghai or Tokyo, but in order to attract foreign investment to Korea, South

Korea has to have some merit. So convenient transport, clean air, and restoring the Cheonggyecheon also makes the air better, making a good place for people to live, a good place to do business. My goal as Seoul's Mayor was to make Seoul Asia's economic center."

Not all stakeholders were on board with the elimination of a major highway to restore a stream that most people remembered as a stinky and polluted eyesore from the 1940s. Most notably, groups working in the area worried about losing their livelihood, and neighborhood associations were afraid of loss of commerce. The resistance to the project decreased as the project's development progressed through the work of the Cheonggyecheon Citizens' Committee. Most criticism of the project after 2005 has been related to the artificial maintenance of the stream and is relatively minimal.

In the end, the plan for Cheonggyecheon restoration was not actually about the stream or the waterway or the traffic. It was about urban renewal. It was about an Asian megacity breaking through the barrier of chaotic, uncontrolled growth to purposeful and resilient city building.

During his time as Mayor, Lee Myung-bak changed the paradigm on both what should be expected from city governments in creating a quality urban experience and also how the people of Seoul interact with their city. This change was the first and pivotal piece in the development of Seoul as a globally recognized smart city.

Key Takeaways:

- *The Cheonggyecheon Restoration Project was controversial at the beginning. The project was ultimately successful because it brought biodiversity back to the city center, decreased the heat island effect in downtown Seoul, and revitalized the local economy.*

- *The restoration of Cheonggyecheon has helped to improve the quality of life for the people of Seoul in a number of ways, and it is a shining example of how urban renewal projects can improve the way people live in cities.*

- *A nature-based urban renewal project is a major undertaking that requires planning and coordination of conflicting interests of various stakeholders, as well as strong leadership from the Mayor.*

TURNING SEOUL INTO A GLOBAL CULTURE CAPITAL

Chapter 6

Political Rookie Oh Se-hoon Takes the Lead

Oh Se-hoon is the quintessential Seoulite: sophisticated and self-assured. Even as a politician in his 60s, he comes across as cool and confident. At a height of over 6 ft with an elegant and modern style, he became a member of the National Assembly for the first time at age 40 and brought a youthful presence to the government of South Korea. He was once named Korea's best dressed politician. He even participated in an ecological fashion show as a model in 2022. Exuding a healthy and outgoing image, he gained popularity through activities like commuting by bicycle along the Han River and playing the drum for the opening of a Seoul Music Festival. Before Oh Se-hoon, Koreans were accustomed to the conservative and authoritative *older statesmen* style of Korean politicians. Early on, he became a representative of the "new Seoul"and a reference for the fashionable Seoulites that would become world famous for their polished aesthetic starting in the early 2000s.

Of the three mayors, he was the only one who was actually born, raised, and spent most of his life in Seoul. He is often mistaken as a member of an elite family because of his public image and dynamic career trajectory. An accomplished academic with credentials from Korea's top universities, Oh Se-hoon started his career as a successful environmental lawyer before becoming a

TV personality. He is also one of the first top-level Korean politicians to be fluent in English.

It is easy to see why people assume he comes from privilege, but Oh Se-hoon is a representative of the new, modern Korea. Over the past two generations, there has been a dynamic shift in the image of Korean people in the world and the way Koreans see themselves. *The Miracle on the Han River* was about the Korean people and their extraordinary ability to unify to adapt to new conditions while taking an active role in their communities and then performing at the next level with confidence and grace. Oh Se-hoon personifies all of these things.

His childhood was no different from that of his peers born in Seoul in the 1960s. He was born in a poor and underdeveloped urban community and witnessed first-hand one of the greatest economic turnarounds of the modern era. Oh Se-hoon was born in a shanty town on Seoul's east side in 1961 and raised by hard-working parents. His father worked for a construction company, and his mother was a seamstress who made blankets to help supplement the family's income. Like Lee Myung-bak, he was a bright and diligent student who also worked to contribute to the family finances. As a child, he once sold ornamental birds such as canaries to help his family make ends meet.

As a determined student in a challenging environment, he entered the law department at Korea University and passed the bar exam in 1984. His early life was relatively normal for a native of Seoul at the time. Oh Se-hoon was part of the first generation in Korea to benefit from the hard-fought dynamic growth of the 1970s and 80s. His success already went far beyond what his parents' generation could ever have dreamed of as a successful private-sector lawyer in a middle-income country. However, fate had more in store for him. In 1994, he took on a case that would signal his rise to national fame as an urban reformer and a defender of citizen's rights.

At age 33, he achieved a first and historic victory in a case about urban residents' right to natural sunlight under the Korean constitution. Seoul underwent a massive transformation in the 1980s and early 1990s, with the removal of many single-story dwellings and the construction of high-rise apartment buildings to alleviate the severe housing shortage from the era of rapid growth in the city. A side-effect of high-rise apartment construction was diminished views and blocked sunlight for neighboring buildings. At the time, Koreans were unfamiliar with the concept of environmental rights and most people were only concerned with owning a comfortable, modern home. While people complained when new construction projects blocked their view or the light in their apartment, they did not really believe that they had the *right* to sunlight and that this right could be guaranteed by law. Oh Se-hoon took on this case and cited an Article of the Korean Constitution in court that 'everyone has the right to live in a healthy and comfortable environment.' He argued that residents should be compensated for lost views and decreased sunlight, and he won the case. Since this was an issue that directly affected the quality of life of many Seoulites, this lawsuit made him famous as an urban reformer.

The success of the lawsuit thrust him into a new world as a national public figure. This development opened up new opportunities and pulled him toward a career in public service. He was invited to host a TV program dealing with social issues, which raised his public profile even more. Later, at age 40, he ran and was elected as a congressman to the National Assembly, representing one of the wealthiest and most exclusive districts in Seoul.

Six years after he entered politics, he became the mayor of Seoul in 2006. But it wasn't the usual case. Oh Se-hoon had stepped away from politics in 2004 after serving as a member of the National Assembly for four years and becoming somewhat disenchanted with the political system. As a reformer in

Korea's right-wing conservative party, he felt that the party's persistent and outdated culture and systems were limiting the growth of the party and expressed as much in an interview when he left his seat in the National Assembly.

"In an era when we have the opportunity to realize important political reform, I actually felt that we moved backwards, away from reform, and I can't help but feel a sense of shame in that reality," he stated.

It was the citizens of Seoul who called him back to public service. In the public polls leading up to the mayoral election in 2006, Oh Se-hoon was chosen as one of the top picks. With some heavy persuasion and the support of his party, the people of Seoul would push him to run for the mayor of Seoul. Only one month before election day, he declared his candidacy for mayor. Despite the short election preparation period, he was elected with over 60% of the votes and took office in 2006. Since 2006, Oh Se-hoon has run for mayor of Seoul four times and has won all the mayoral elections, including by-elections. He served as the mayor of Seoul from 2006 to 2011 for 5 years and returned to the mayor's seat in 2021.

It would not be an overstatement to say that Oh Se-hoon has been a principal player in the development of modern Seoul. He served as the mayor of Seoul over such a long period of time and has had significant influence over the direction of growth of the city. His principal policies involved building on the improved efficiency of his predecessor and creating a recognizable brand identity for Seoul. If the people of Seoul had not intervened and let him leave politics for good, Seoul would surely look different than it does today. In the next three chapters, we will introduce his most significant projects that built Seoul's reputation for design and style while improving quality of life for Seoulites.

Chapter 7

Seoul Becomes a World Design Capital

In 2002, a monumental year for Koreans, South Korea and Japan co-hosted the 2002 FIFA world cup, the first World Cup tournament held in Asia. The Korean team, or *Taegeuk Warriors* (태극전사들), as they were nicknamed in the global media, surprised the world soccer fans by defeating European powerhouse Spain 5-3 on penalties to make it to the semifinals. At the moment when the fame of *The Miracle on the Han River* was fading away, the Korean soccer team's Cinderella performance at the 2002 FIFA World Cup brought back worldwide attention toward South Korea, and the country saw a surge in tourism for a few years. Hallyu (한류), the global wave of Korean pop culture, was also starting to emerge at the time, and that may also have inspired people to visit Korea.

In the early 2000s, what impression would a foreign tourist have had of Seoul? At that time, foreigners were much less familiar with Korean culture than they are now, and Seoul was a less pleasant place for tourists than it is now. Back then, the sidewalks were always crowded with people, and it was hard to breathe because the air was so congested from exhaust fumes from cars. The pedestrian areas at street level were disorienting for foreigners who don't speak Korean because of the exotic and unorganized signs written in Hangul. Monotonous gray apartment complexes resembling obscure-shape matchboxes lined the Han River waterfront. In the eyes of foreigners, Seoul may have looked like a republic of apartments or a concrete jungle. In the end, travelers may have wondered if Seoul is truly the right choice for their costly overseas travel, as there was nothing special to do except visit a few historical sites like Gyeongbokgung Palace and enjoy the vibrant nightlife scene in Myeong-dong, Gangnam station or Insa-dong.

When Oh Se-hoon became Mayor, transforming Seoul into a tourist destination was high on his priority list. He knew that tourism receipts were an important tool to help balance the municipal budget and felt that the Korean capital had a lot to offer international travelers. The city just needed a little polish. He was a strong believer that design was a key in transforming Seoul into an attractive tourist destination.

He stated this position clearly at the opening ceremony of the World Design Cities Summit in February 2010. "Design is everything," Seoul Mayor Oh Se-hoon declared during his speech at the event. "Good design helps local government communicate with its citizens and creates high added value. Ultimately, design is the key to enhancing quality of life."

Whether he intended to or not, Oh Se-hoon has been a champion of beauty and design throughout his political career. After studying urban policy and social sciences on a fellowship at King's College in London, he was inspired to initiate a series of beautification and sustainability projects. Mayor Oh Se-hoon wanted Seoul to become a city like New York that could attract over 47 million global tourists annually and earn billions of dollars in tourism revenue. To achieve this goal, he focused on injecting an element of design into the city by establishing the *Design Seoul Initiative.*

The Design Seoul Initiative was a city-wide beautification project conceptualized to raise the profile of Korea's capital city. Since Seoul was a city where nature and tradition coexisted, he felt that the transition from developing to developed nation capital required more comprehensive design solutions. Oh Se-hoon reasoned that just as people from around the world visit New York to tour the Statue of Liberty and Wall Street, Barcelona for La Sagrada Familia, or Paris for the Eiffel Tower and the Louvre, he could transform Seoul into a globally attractive city with the promotion of *design*.

Because he believed so strongly that design was the key to transforming Seoul into a city like New York, he first carried out organizational reform to better enable the transformation. He established a brand-new department to oversee and manage the overall design of the city of Seoul.

The first action was to introduce *design* as a means to transform Seoul into a beautiful city. From an urban design point of view, the cityscapes in Seoul in the 2000s were a disaster. At that time, overcrowded, chaotic and ugly signage severely damaged Seoul's landscape. Storefront signage in 2006 was relatively large compared to the size of the stores themselves, and the words were very tightly packed with inconsistent spacing. The lettering was also somewhat vulgar in red, blue, yellow or green and mostly in oversized, gothic script. The design of city infrastructure, such as sidewalks, street lights, waste bins, and bus stops, had the same problems as the signage. Because this city infrastructure had been produced and installed focusing only on function, little thought had been given to the characteristics of materials or colors used. Public facilities that were installed without regard for overall design were another major blight on the streets of Seoul. In May 2008, Mayor Oh announced the *Seoul Public Design Guidelines* for public spaces, public buildings, public facilities, public visual media, and night scenery to unify and update the overall aesthetic of the city of Seoul.

The second action was to create attractive destinations in Seoul. Oh Se-hoon felt that the charm of New York was not limited to tourist attractions such as the Empire State Building and the Statue of Liberty but also the city's cultural offerings, such as world-class art museums and theater performances. He was especially inspired by a case study of The Bilbao Effect[18]. Bilbao is a city in the Basque Country on the Atlantic Coast of Spain with a population of 350,000. It was principally a mining and port city that had been in decline for decades before the Guggenheim Museum opened in 1997 as the centerpiece of the city government's revitalization plan. Bilbao now punches far above its weight in cultural tourism, welcoming over a million tourists annually and generating over US$2 billion from tourism. The case of Bilbao motivated him to initiate multiple construction projects under his visionary slogan of *Design Seoul*. The Dongdaemun Design Plaza (DDP) is one of the marquee projects initiated under the Design Seoul mandate.

DDP bird's eye view
(Source: Seoul Metropolitan Government)

---

[18] After witnessing Bilbao's success, people have coined the term 'the Bilbao Effect' indicating when cities use powerful architecture to revitalize or boost the local economy.

DDP at night
(Source: Seoul Metropolitan Government)

DDP at night
(Source: Seoul Metropolitan Government)

In the beginning, citizens of the city were not excited about the DDP project. The site of DDP is in a neighborhood with a long and significant history for Seoulites as it was the location of the eastern gate of Seoul, built at the beginning of the Joseon dynasty in 1396. It was a major thoroughfare in the city for centuries before a sports stadium was built there during the Japanese occupation. Dongdaemun Stadium became a central landmark for the city in the post-war years and was the site of many events related to the national identity of South Korea, such as national sports festivals, Miss Korea contests and baseball games. Because of the central role the stadium played as the location of Korean national events, there was sentimental attachment to the stadium.

There was another reason why Mayor Oh chose the Dongdaemun Stadium site as the design hub of Seoul. The DDP site was next to Korea's two historical fashion hubs –Pyounghwa Market (평화시장) and Dongdaemun Market (동대문시장). The markets created a garment district with over 2,500 stores, where people can find everything from fabrics and accessories to finished products like clothes and shoes. Pyounghwa Market started as an informal market after the Korean War and grew as the Korean fashion industry expanded. Dongdaemun Market came later in 1970 and opened as Asia's largest clothing market in a 3-story building covering over a million sq ft. The area grew into a full-fledged fashion district in 1999 with the opening of a brand-new 34-story modern building filled with fashion shops at Dongdaemun Market. For Mayor Oh, the Dongdaemun Stadium site seemed like an ideal place to locate a landmark building to establish Seoul as a design hub.

DDP was designed by Zaha Hadid, a British-Iranian architect known for her vision of radical deconstructionism, with local partner *Samoo Architects & Engineers*[19]. The building has a unique exterior design resembling a spaceship with rounded sides and a cantilever structure. DDP is a multi-use building that includes a museum, shopping, restaurants, exhibition and event space, and outdoor gardens. What makes the building

---

[19.] Samoo is one of Samsung Group's affiliate companies and closely working with Samsung C&T Corporation.

truly unique is not only the number of open and airy passageways and meeting spaces but also the design details that include a curated furniture collection.

In preparation for the 1986 Asian Games and the 1988 Seoul Olympics, the Korean government built a new sports complex in a different location, *Jamsil Sports Complex* (잠실종합운동장). Dongdaemun Stadium and its surrounding area started to seem outdated. Lee Myung-bak's Cheonggyecheon Restoration Project resulted in speeding up the deterioration of the area as street vendors that once occupied the area around Cheonggyecheon flocked to the unused space in Dongdaemun Stadium to set up an informal market on the stadium field. As soon as Oh Se-hoon took office, he launched the plan for the renovation of the Dongdaemun area. The demolition work of Dongdaemun Stadium began in 2007, one year after he took office. Construction started in 2009, and DDP opened to the public five years later in 2014. DDP immediately became a landmark in Seoul, visited by about 14 million people in 2015.

DDP served as Oh Se-hoon's declaration to the world of Seoul's new role as a capital of design and culture, a theme he has built on further throughout his career. The timing of this project perfectly complemented the rise of Korean culture on the global scene and has reinforced the image of Seoul as a chic and modern city.

The third action was to foster the design industry in Seoul. Oh Se-hoon hoped that building DDP would function both as a global tourist destination and a center for the creative design industry. To complement the DDP construction in 2009, Mayor Oh Se-hoon launched the Seoul Design Foundation, and he was successful in getting Seoul designated as a 2010 UNESCO Creative City for design[20]. After the completion and opening of the DDP building, the Seoul Design Foundation

---

[20]. The UNESCO Creative Cities Network (UCCN) was created in 2004 to promote cooperation among cities that have identified creativity as a strategic factor for sustainable urban development.

opened a start-up center to nurture the design industry and launched an annual festival called *Seoul Design Week*[21] in 2014. As Seoul's representative design event, *Seoul Design Week* includes events like design exhibitions and markets along with Seoul's design "hotspot" tour programs. He also created knowledge platforms to make Seoul a meeting place for design professionals, such as the *Herald Design Forum*, where key stakeholders in the space discuss the future of design, and *Design Talks* featuring key players on the design scene in Seoul.

Mayor Oh Se-hoon has successfully turned Seoul into a clean and attractive city with many things to see and do. His vision and leadership have been key in transforming the face of Seoul by focusing on marquee interventions like DDP as well as small details in the urban fabric that make a big difference in user experience. This difference originated from an effort to focus on people-centered design and is felt in the way both foreigners and locals interact with the city. As we will discuss in the last chapter, Oh Se-hoon continues to strive to improve Seoul's design strategy and maintain its position as a global leader in people-centric design.

Key Takeaways:

- *Mayor Oh Se-hoon is a strong believer that design is key to transforming Seoul into an attractive tourist destination.*

- *He introduced the Seoul Public Design Guidelines, constructed the Dongdaemun Design Plaza, and established the Seoul Design Foundation to achieve this goal.*

- *These initiatives have helped to make Seoul a global design hub and have put the city on the global map as a center for design and innovation.*

---

[21] For more information, visit https://seoul-design.or.kr/

Chapter 8

Reborn as a Waterfront City

The Han River is one of the first landmarks people see when they arrive in Seoul. The main roads from Incheon International Airport to the center of Seoul are the Gangbyeon Expressway (강변북로) and Olympic Expressway (올림픽대로), both of which run parallel to the Han River and offer generous views of the river during most of the ride to downtown Seoul. On the way, visitors can see high-rise buildings and apartments built along the Han River during the daytime and the illuminated bridges connecting Gangbuk and Gangnam at night.

The Miracle on the Han River has come to be known worldwide as the spectacular transformation from one of the poorest countries in the world to one of the 10 largest economies in the world over a span of about 50 years. Comparing pictures of the Han River from different times, one in the 1960s and the other in the 2000s, can help visualize Korea's remarkable development story. The scenery of the Han River and its surroundings have changed dramatically from riverside areas with floating stores and homes, where women washed clothes or children splashed in the water to a developed area with parks and sports facilities surrounded by modern buildings.

The Han River is not just a symbol of South Korea's rapid economic growth, it also played a significant role in bringing about the modernization of Seoul. The river served as a

**©Han Youngsoo_Hangang River, Seoul 1956-1963_
Courtesy Han Youngsoo Foundation**

Han River Scenery in Seoul
(Source: Seoul Research Data Service)

The Han River, with a width of about 1 km, is the second-largest river in
South Korea. The road on the left is Olympic Expressway,
and on the right is Gangbyeon Expressway.

starting point from which the national highway network was developed, leading to major ports such as Incheon and Busan. The government also looked to the Han River to find a solution to the growing pains experienced during the period of rapid growth in South Korea. Land was reclaimed from the river for the development of new towns located to the south of the Han River, in the area of Gangnam.

Gangnam Style is one of the phrases that come to mind when people around the world think about South Korea. People may not know anything about the area or understand any of the lyrics of the song by Psy that made the district of Seoul famous, but they know that the residents of the Gangnam district in Seoul are cool (and a little bit flashy). The song *Gangnam Style* was the first in a series of high-profile Korean cultural works[22] to be accepted *en masse* on the global scene and is very much related to the urban development policy of the city of Seoul over the past 50 years. As outlined in Chapter 2, Gangnam is the name of the districts located south of the Han River that was built up in the 1970s as part of the plan to modernize Seoul. As South Korea's economic development plan accelerated, there was a mass movement of people to the capital, and this created a massive housing shortage, which the local government sought to resolve by the creation and build out of Gangnam. Today, the Gangnam neighborhood has become the face of Seoul globally, with luxury boutiques, high-rise buildings, cool coffee shops, and very fashionable people.

Even with the importance the Han River played as a resource in the development of the city, it also fell victim to Korea's economic growth for a number of years. The natural beach along the river was a popular spot for Seoul citizens to enjoy

---

[22] Psy's *Gangnam Style* became a global hit in 2012. In the ten years that followed, Korean entertainment soared to great heights with international boy band and cultural phenomenon BTS breaking records for pop music across the globe, the first non-English-language Best Picture Oscar going to Bong Joon Ho's movie 'Parasite' in 2020 and the Netflix series 'Squid Game' became the streaming service's most watched series globally in 2021.

swimming and bathing in the summer in the 1950s and 60s. Along the Han River, there were wide sand dunes where people relaxed and enjoyed picnics. As development ramped up in the 1970s, the beach virtually disappeared and the water was polluted with industrial and domestic waste runoff.

During preparations for the 1986 Asian Games and 1988 Summer Olympic Games, people once again started to pay closer attention to the riverside area. The government started to think of the Han River as a significant part of the landscape of Seoul and treated it with more care and respect. With the pressure of a massive number of foreign arrivals for the two global events, the Korean government embarked on an extensive redevelopment project for the Han River and the surrounding area. Included in this project was the building of four sewage treatment plants to purify the river water and the installation of concrete banks along the river to prevent flooding. The redevelopment also included the creation of protected public parks in areas where sandy beaches and wetlands still existed. Sports facilities, such as soccer and basketball courts, were built in the riverside area, and parking lots were created to enable access to the new riverside facilities. Where the sand dunes were gone for good, concrete facilities were built that enabled people to enjoy the riverside ambiance. Although different from its former state as a place where Seoulites could enjoy nature, the Han River was revived as a popular destination where many citizens visited to enjoy the outdoors and escape the summer heat.

Although people started to return to the Han River area for leisure outings, it did not necessarily mean they considered the Han River a beautiful or pleasant destination. In the 1990s, the Han River area became known as a leisure park where families enjoyed walking, exercising, and even fishing, but only during the daytime. At night, the situation changed as there were few streetlights, which turned the Han River area into a sketchy area with higher rates of criminal activities. In addition, the Han River earned a reputation as a suicide spot. In

Korean, the expression "I go to the Han River" has come to mean that a person is struggling with suicidal thoughts and feels hopeless.

At the Han River Park in Spring
(Source: Seoul Research Data Service)

Bicycle paths have been installed along the Han River, and the number of cyclists in the area has exploded.

Building on the redevelopment of the Han River area during the 1980s and 90s, as well as the redevelopment of Cheonggyecheon in the mid-2000s, Oh Se-hoon developed a plan to completely transform the riverside area. He launched The Han River Renaissance Project in 2006 as part of his agenda to beautify the city of Seoul. Mayor Oh Se-hoon envisioned the Han River as a nature-based solution to transform Seoul into a sustainable waterfront city. Mayor Oh's administration set forth a spending plan of over 500 billion KRW (about US$ 412 million) over four years from 2006 to 2010 to beautify the space and make it more attractive and accessible to locals as well as visitors to the city. He carried out the four principal interventions.

1.   Improving accessibility

Mayor Oh created a 78 km long bicycle-only road and walking trail along the Han River and increased passageways connecting the Han Riverfront. Because of the way in which the riverside and local highway network were originally developed, options for pedestrian access were extremely limited. Before Oh Se-hoon's reforms the most convenient way, by far, for people to go to the riverside area was by car. The main entries of the Han River Parks were commonly through exits off the highways. To resolve this issue, the government built a number of bridges over the freeway and tunnels under the freeway to make the river accessible to walkers.

2.   Restoring the ecological environment

Ecological parks along the riverside were developed or expanded under the Project. The parks started to provide citizens with something more memorable than just escaping the heat. The government of Seoul started to plant flowers and vines on the concrete revetments and retaining walls along the Han River. Endangered animals like otters and wildcats also started to appear around the Han River. According to a recent report, the number of trees and the number of living species in the Han River area has increased by 300% since the launch of the Han River Renaissance Project. The ecological improvements in the Han River area garnered international attention, leading to Seoul being honored with the Award for the Most Environmentally Sustainable Project in a Built Environment at the 2010 Livcom Awards. The Livcom Awards (https://www.livcomawards.com/) are international awards that recognize achievements in environmental sustainability and the development of liveable communities.

Sebitseom Island
(Source: The Seoul Research Data Service)

3.   Creating cultural destinations

Even until the early 2000s, the only tourist destination related to the Han River was a cruise ship tour program that had opened in 1986. Mayor Oh launched an online citizen engagement platform in 2006 known as the Oasis of 10 Million Imagination (천만상상오아시스), aimed at gathering innovative policy or planning suggestions from residents. One of the proposals on the Oasis platform suggested the creation of a 'floating island' to enhance the city's touristic offering. Oh Se-hoon and the Seoul administration embraced the concept, resulting in the development of Sebitseom (세빛섬). Sebitseom is a series of three floating islands on the river that have been developed into commercial and event spaces for citizens and tourists. As the world's inaugural floating architectural structure, Sebitseom emerged as a pivotal component of the Han River Renaissance Project. Although the project cost 96.4 billion KRW (about US$86 million) to build, Seoul taxpayer money was not used. Sebitseom was constructed by a private company on the condition of a Build-Operate-Transfer (BOT) contract that stipulated that it would be returned to Seoul after 20 years of operation. The sites are tremendously popular, with an average of 4,500 daily visitors on weekdays and 10 thousand visitors on weekends. Sebitseom's distinctive design even earned it a feature in one of the *Avengers* movies.

4.   Beautify the Landscape

The Han River Renaissance Project made the bridges over the river a centerpiece for the beautification of the city. The nighttime illumination along the river is now an iconic scene in Seoul. The government first illuminated seven principle bridges and then continued to expand the illumination plan to the rest of the bridges in the city. The Moonlight Rainbow Fountains at Banpo Hangang Park, featured in the Guinness Book of World Records as the longest bridge fountain in the world, was implemented through this Han River Renaissance Project. From April to October, the fountain puts on a 20-minute show for visitors with 200 multicolored lights and music. The idea of Moonlight Rainbow Fountains was proposed by a Seoul public official.

The Han River Renaissance Project has played a pivotal role in advancing the efforts initiated during the administration of Lee Myung-bak to establish Seoul as a global city. Much of the achievement of this project was not only due to the skill in urban planning by the Oh Se-hoon administration but also by his policy of public consultation in creating the plans. Two essential public consultation mechanisms ensured that the project stayed balanced and represented a diversity of interests and needs for the community:

a.   The Hangang Renaissance Citizens Committee – a 27-member committee dedicated to outreach to the public. This committee is composed of local stakeholders such as members of local non-profit

Banpo Moonlight Rainbow Fountain
(Source: Seoul Research Data Service)

organizations as well as members of city council, and they look into topics related to planning, environment and security, history and culture, and life and traffic. This committee is pivotal to adapting to the changing environment as well as assessing and implementing public suggestions.

b. Oasis of 10 million Imagination Portal – a website that allows the public to submit ideas to the municipal government for public improvement. Since its launch in 2006, the Oasis Portal has garnered over 16,000 ideas and quite a few of these ideas have been integrated into official policies. Among the numerous ideas submitted by Seoul citizens were proposals to enhance the Han River Parks, including concepts for Sebitsoem Islands and the establishment of the Han River Forest Trails, both of which eventually became integral components of the Han River Renaissance Project.

Beyond these two formal mechanisms for public engagement, there are a number of public organizations that are involved in the upkeep and maintenance of the Han River area. Some groups regularly do garbage collection while others plant trees, but public engagement with the area is high and growing. Following the success of the public engagement campaigns launched for the Cheonggyecheon Restoration Project, this aspect of the Han River Renaissance Project has been central to the overall plan. Pivotal to the development of Seoul as a sustainable city has been the idea that private citizens must be consulted on a regular basis to make sure it is a people-oriented community.

Today, the Han River Park has become a pleasant place where residents of Seoul gather daily. Like downtown Cheonggyecheon, office workers enjoy walking along the Han River during their lunch break. On the weekends, the Han River's 78 km-long bike path is crowded with cyclists. Various events, such as local marathons, night markets, and free concerts, provide a variety of things to see and enjoy in the waterfront area. Oh Se-hoon's signature project has brought about a new glory to Korea's iconic Han River.

Key Takeaways:

- *The Han River is a symbol of South Korea's rapid economic growth and played a significant role in the modernization of Seoul.*

- *The Han River Renaissance Project has included the construction of new parks, bridges, and cultural attractions and helped to improve the ecological environment of the river.*

- *The Han River Renaissance Project has made the river a more attractive and accessible place for locals and visitors alike. Citizen consultation and collaboration has been key to the success of the project.*

Chapter 9
Tackling the Equitable Housing Conundrum

For many people around the world, the dream of making it in the big city is getting further away. Urban life is costly. The purchase of property in any major metropolitan area like New York, London or Hong Kong starts in the millions of dollars and has become an exclusive privilege of high net-worth individuals and those with generational wealth. Even rental apartments in a major city cost upwards of US$5,000 per month, and that budget does not necessarily guarantee a brand-new or spacious living space. City residents without access to this level of income are forced to move farther outside the urban area, requiring longer commuting times and often smaller and run-down conditions. In absolute terms, Seoul seems to be slightly better than New York in finding affordable homes. However, if you look at the situation in real terms, Seoul housing costs have also skyrocketed out of reach for most local residents. The average price of an apartment in Seoul is over US$1 million, an impossible sum for most people that would require them to save all of their income for many years to afford. As a result, skyrocketing housing prices have contributed to the population outflow from Seoul. An average of 480,000 people move to the neighboring areas of Incheon and Gyeonggi province every year, and the city's population has consistently declined since reaching over 10 million in 1988.

Seoul with high-rise apartment blocks
(Source: Seoul Metropolitan Government)

More than half of Korean households
live in apartments. The majority of
Koreans still dream of owning an apartment in Seoul.

From a city management perspective, a population decrease in an overcrowded megacity like Seoul may not necessarily be bad. The decreased population can reduce social overhead costs like schools, hospitals, and roads, but a population decrease resulting from the majority of the population being priced out of the city alters the fabric of the city and makes it more exclusive and less diverse. Runaway housing costs diminish urban equity levels and chip away at the overall quality of life in the city.

From the point of view of the average citizen, moving out of the urban area can have high opportunity costs. Seoul promises good-quality education, jobs, and medical care. The college entrance rate of high school students from Seoul is twice as high as students from other provinces. Most of Korea's top 100 companies have headquarters in Seoul, so the management-and top-level jobs in those companies are only available in Seoul. The top-ranked hospitals and doctors with a wide variety of expertise are also located in Seoul. Giving up life in Seoul inevitably means giving up on all of the things the capital city has to offer. Because there is such a strong concentration of activity there, leaving Seoul can have significant implications on one's life journey.

Traditionally, the real estate market in South Korea has a unique model for rental contracts called the Jeonse system (전세)[23]. The system dates back over a century and was created as a solution to a lack of mortgage lending in a dynamically growing economy. The idea is that when a dwelling is made available to renters, the renters give the owners a deposit equivalent to 50 to 80% of the dwelling's value and then live there rent-free for two years. Because the deposit is so large, the owner of the dwelling can use this money for other purposes for two years, such as investing the money or putting it into high-interest savings accounts. The renter can also take advantage of two years of rent-free living to save and prepare a larger deposit or even a mortgage down-payment. At the end of the contract, the deposit can be renegotiated, and the contract can be extended. In practice, a renter in the Jeonse system would have some savings and could get a Jeonse loan from the bank to cover the remainder of what they need for the deposit. As down payments for mortgages in South Korea tend to be higher than they are in the West at around 50 to 70% of the purchase price, Jeonse has been a viable alternative for people who do not yet possess the cash to get a mortgage loan for a housing purchase, and has been used extensively in high-priced Seoul.

The Jeonse system also has several disadvantages. Even

[23.] *Renting a House in South Korea: Jeonse* (n.d.). Asia Society. https://asiasociety.org/korea/renting-house-south-korea-jeonse

though the renter can obtain a home on a budget below market price, it does not eliminate the renter's housing insecurity. Since the Jeonse contract period is two years, there is the possibility that the homeowner will discontinue the contract every two years. Even if the contract is renewed, homeowners often ask for an additional deposit, and sometimes a substantial one. Housing prices in a city of such dynamic growth as Seoul are constantly increasing, and the increase in home values can result in a drastic increase in the Jeonse deposit from one 2-year contract cycle to the next. This can put renters in a difficult position and require them to move every two years in search of a more affordable Jeonse agreement. People who do not have enough savings for a Joense deposit are forced to take the most undesirable dwellings like the well-known example of the below-street-level apartment featured in the 2019 Oscar-winning movie *Parasite*.

Public housing, often called social housing or affordable housing in Western countries, is an option in Seoul that the Korean government first made available to low-income residents starting in 1971. Initially, public housing was offered only to households in urgent need, such as those living in the

Typical Floor Designs of Affordable Housing In Korea
(Source: Korea Land and Housing Corporation)

informal housing settlements that were being cleared to make way for new developments during the reconstruction boom, evicted residents, or displaced persons. As economic growth started giving way to the development of formal high-rises, the number of people needing housing assistance increased, and policies were created to help low-income people find affordable housing. However, the public program was designed only for low-income residents, and the housing units under the program were mostly small, like single-studio or one-bedroom units.

Shortly after Oh Se-hoon took office in 2006, the world economy descended into chaos and took South Korea with it. Global markets, led by real estate fraud and a mortgage crisis, plummeted, and Seoul was no exception. A critical risk in the Jeonse system is that if the real estate market crashes, there may be an unfortunate situation in which the homeowner is unable to return the Jeonse deposit to the renter. With the onset of the global financial crisis in 2007, many homeowners lost the ability to pay back the Jeonse deposit they had invested. The low and middle-income classes in Seoul were gravely affected, and the renters became victims of the homeowners' default on Jeonse deposits.

Recalling memories of having to move often when he was young because of Jeonse deposits that spiraled beyond his family's reach, Oh Se-hoon looked for a way to provide more stable housing options for the people of Seoul. Oh Se-hoon had grown up poor at a time when affordable housing policies did not exist in South Korea. He understood the feeling of hopelessness and desperation associated with housing insecurity. He felt that the right to stable housing is a basic building block for a sustainable city, so he was determined to improve the long-term public housing rental program for Seoul citizens.

As the dynamic growth of the city of Seoul created a situation in which the rise in housing costs far outpaced the rise in salaries, Mayor Oh paid attention to the fact that middle-income families were increasingly leaving Seoul. It led him to devise an unprecedented new public housing program called the SHIFT program, especially targeting middle-class families in need of some housing assistance. Under this program, the people of Seoul are able to rent mid-to-large-sized apartments with a Jeonse deposit at a price 20% lower than the surrounding market price. The program also stipulates that Jeonse contracts can be extended for up to 20 years, with deposit increases capped at 5% every two years. The SHIFT program is focused on giving stability to working families, and one of the principal reasons for the introduction of the program was to provide an opportunity for families in Seoul to raise their children in Seoul's educational environment without concerns over housing insecurity. With contracts available to extend up to 20 years, the SHIFT program ensures that families have enough time in the urban environment for long-term educational planning.

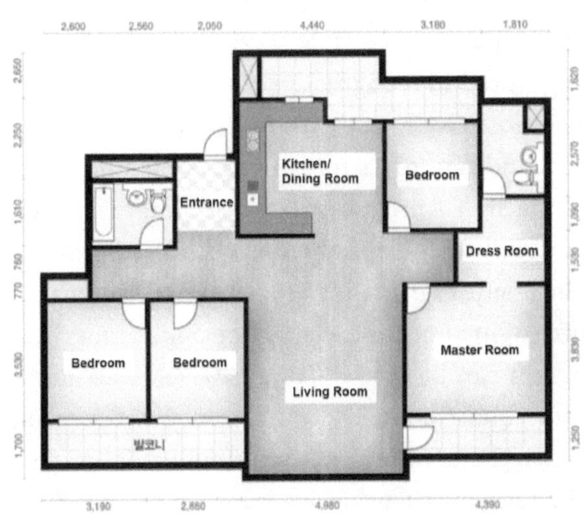

**An example of Apartment Floor Designs
Under Seoul SHIFT program**
(Source: Seoul Housing & Communities Corporation)

In January 2007, the Seoul Metropolitan Government announced a long-term Jeonse housing program and a promise to supply 24,000 units by March 2010. The program was popular, with the first round bringing in over 225,000 applicants or 10 applicants applying for every available apartment. As of June 2020, the SHIFT program has announced housing application openings for a total of 38 rounds, and it has become a cornerstone of the Mayor's fight to maintain some level of equity for low- and middle-income families in the overheated Seoul real estate market.

The program has also received international recognition. In 2010, Seoul's SHIFT program received the most prestigious award in the field of human habitation worldwide from UN-Habitat, a United Nations affiliate. During her visit to Seoul to present the award, UN Under-Secretary-General and Secretary-General of UN-Habitat, Anna Tibaizuka, remarked on how the UN's vision is to ensure affordable housing and provide it at an accessible cost. She emphasized that "the award was granted in recognition of the SHIFT program's exemplary and innovative nature, deserving promotion."

In addition to its role in providing affordable housing in the city, the SHIFT program plays a second role in securing the city's financial future. Not only does the SHIFT program function as a tool to fight housing inequity in Seoul, but it is also a long-term source of income for the city. The public units built for the SHIFT program can be sold off after 20 years at market value, which would almost certainly bring a very hefty profit. These profits can then be used to fund other public programs in the city. It is an investment that the city is making in itself.

The city budget in Seoul has been steadily increasing. The 2022 budget allocated for the Seoul Metropolitan Government was approximately 44 trillion KRW (US$40 billion). How much a local government is able to transform their city into a smarter, more sustainable city or implement brand-new smart city services is closely related to the financial capability of the city. Smart city services are costly because they generally require uninterrupted operation and regular technological advancement. The city of Seoul has the highest degree of financial independence among Korean cities. While most Korean cities are less than 50% financially self-sufficient, Seoul is a city that manages 77% of its finances through its tax collections. As a result, Seoul is inevitably last in line for financial support to promote innovative projects such as smart city interventions. Potential revenue-producing programs like SHIFT have become fundamental in balancing the city budget and making continued progress in the sustainable development of Seoul.

Affordable housing and diversity in urban areas is sure to be one of the great global conundrums of the 21st century. Every city in the world is grappling with how to keep a diversity of residents in their homes while maintaining a robust property market under the capitalist system. Runaway housing prices are as much a problem in Seoul as they are anywhere else, but by taking a long-term view, the government of Seoul has found a way to relieve some pressure on the lower-income population in the city while sowing the seeds for future solutions. There is certainly much more work to be done to bring more affordable housing solutions to Seoul, but the SHIFT program has created a solution for working families and a toolbox for future generations.

Key Takeaways:

- *The rise in housing costs in Seoul has made it almost impossible for many people to afford to live in the city.*

- *The SHIFT program is a long-term housing program that provides affordable housing to middle-class families in Seoul, and it serves as an investment mechanism for the city government.*

- *The SHIFT program is a successful example of how a local government can intervene in the housing market to provide affordable housing and secure its financial future.*

PART IV

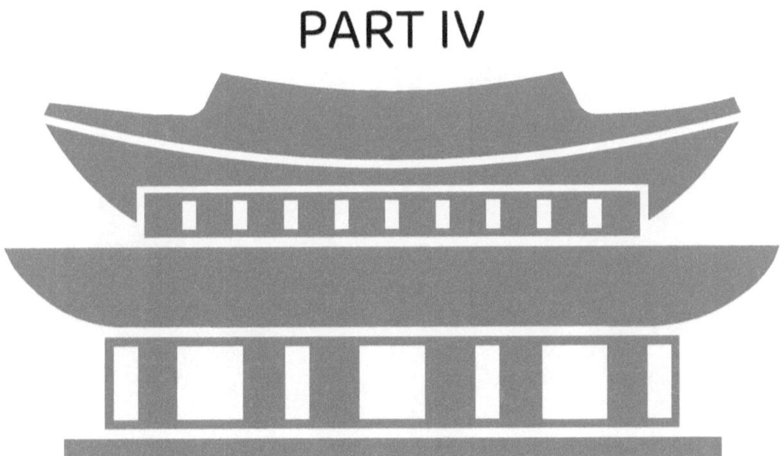

SHAPING A
SHARING CITY

Chapter 10

Activist Park Won-soon's Challenge for Seoul

Park Won-soon was not a politician. He eventually became one of the most important and well-known elected officials in South Korea, but it was social activism that pulled him into the political arena. In fact, Park Won-soon only ever held the post of Mayor of Seoul, an elected post that is widely considered the second most powerful position in South Korea. Both unusual and highly effective, Park Won-soon offered an alternative route to development that incorporated higher levels of community and traditional Korean cultural values.

Park Won-soon didn't just come from obscurity to hold one of the highest offices in the country; he had built a reputation and a career on building philanthropic culture and making strides toward leveling the playing field for all members of Korean society. He was the founder of two important community-based organizations that had a dynamic effect on Korean society during the transition decades of the 1990s and 2000s: The People's Solidarity for Participatory Democracy (PSPD, 참여연대) and The Beautiful Foundation (아름다운재단).

The PSPD was a non-profit dedicated to rooting out political corruption and building a participatory democracy. It was established in 1994 and played an important role in South Korea's transformation from an authoritarian regime to a democratic society through grassroots-driven activities that aimed to bring more transparency to the Korean political and economic system. The PSPD played an instrumental role in passing the Anti-Corruption Act by successfully carrying out a signature campaign and had a hand in convincing the OECD evaluating committee that the tolerance for corruption in South Korea had decreased significantly from the 1970s. Shareholder activism was also a focus, and the PSPD played a pivotal role in bringing more transparency to the corporate decision-making process in the years following the Asian Financial Crisis. Wherever issues of corruption were creating roadblocks in the advancement of Korean society, the PSPD worked to eliminate them.

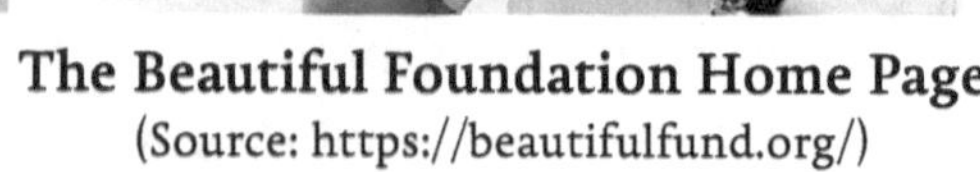

The Beautiful Foundation Home Page
(Source: https://beautifulfund.org/)

As a non-profit foundation created by citizens, Park Won-soon contributed greatly to establishing and stabilizing the Foundation.

The second organization founded by Park Won-soon is The Beautiful Foundation (https://beautifulfund.org/). The Beautiful Foundation, established in 2000, was the first social enterprise in South Korea to focus on building a culture of philanthropy among ordinary citizens. In the 1980s and the 1990s, foundations in South Korea were generally regarded as institutions operated by corporations for tax reduction or for the hiding of their wealth. For this reason, large foundations were viewed with distrust and suspicion, and donation culture on an organized level had remained weak in South Korea. The Beautiful Foundation flipped this perception. It was a grass-roots organization that was founded without the support of any major stakeholders like corporations or high net-worth individuals. The foundation has changed Korean's perception toward foundations and boosted the citizen-led philanthropic culture in South Korea.

As a founding member of both PSPD and the Beautiful Foundation, Park Won-soon was well known in political cir-cles as a proponent of transparency in democracy and promot-ing public interest and inclusion in the societal landscape. Building strong community bonds was one of his main objec-tives and, until he ran for political office, participation in non-profit activities was his tool of preference for community-building.

Park Won-soon, like Lee Myung-bak and Oh Se-hoon, grew up poor. However, unlike the other two, he was a country kid who didn't come to Seoul until he became a teenager. Born in 1955 as the sixth of seven children to a peasant farmer, he spent his youth in ChangNyeong (창녕), which is in the south-ern part of the Korean peninsula between Daegu (대구) and Busan (부산). His hometown had a population of about 15,000 and was surrounded by mountains and rivers. He didn't have electricity until he entered middle school, and he had to travel about 12 kilometers every day to attend school.

In 1970, he moved to Seoul by himself when he was just 15. He left his family to study at the prestigious Kyunggi High School (경기고등학교) in Seoul, and after that he was admit-ted to South Korea's top-ranked university, Seoul National University (SNU, 서울대학교). SNU has mythic status in South Korea, similar to Harvard or Princeton in the United States. But even as an academic overachiever, he could not escape the turbulent times in which he lived. He did not graduate from

SNU because he was expelled for being involved in a political incident related to political activism. This was not unusual under Park Chung-hee's military regime. Many college students were expelled or forcibly sent to the military when they were perceived to be participating in any type of anti-government activities.

Undeterred, Park finished his undergraduate degree at Dankook University (단국대학교), one of the high-ranking universities located in Seoul. He passed the bar exam in 1980 and, two years later in 1982, became a public prosecutor in Daegu, South Korea's fourth largest city, which is near his hometown. However, he did not feel comfortable with the prosecutor's duties of imprisoning, punishing, or attending executions and resigned after one year to become a human rights lawyer. Park came onto the national scene when he got involved in the fight to seek recognition from Japan for human rights violations from the Japanese occupation of Korea from 1910 until the end of World War II. Most notably, he worked to prosecute cases on behalf of 'comfort women (정신대),' Korean women and girls who were forced into sexual slavery by the Japanese Imperial Army both before and during WWII. He was also a lawyer in a monumental case for the promotion of women's rights in South Korea. In 1986, there was an incident in which a female college student went undercover to investigate the treatment of women at the labor site. She was discovered, arrested, and was sexually tortured by the police chief. With the help of a team of human rights lawyers, including Park Won-soon, she filed a complaint against the police in an effort to stop sexual torture and harassment by public officers. In a male-dominated culture where women were often mistreated, the lawsuit drew a lot of attention, especially when they won the case.

Park Won-soon was the chairman of the Beautiful Foundation when he threw his hat in the ring for the 2011 Seoul mayoral by-election as an independent. The opportunity arose when

Mayor Oh Se-hoon resigned before completing his second term as mayor. Seoul had to hold a by-election to replace him, and Park decided to run. The election of Park Won-soon was heralded as a new phase in Korean politics. It was an unprecedented event that the Office of the Mayor in South Korea's capital and largest city was given to a man representing no political parties and known as a community activist and promoter of volunteerism.

His nine-year tenure (2011–2020) as Mayor of Seoul was the longest of the democratic era. His accomplishments are, however, somewhat lower-profile than those that Lee Myung-bak and Oh Se-hoon were able to boast. In part, this is because he was an anti-developmentist. He focused more on advocating and supporting the creation of sustainable communities and the restoration of historic or underdeveloped areas through a range of urban renewal projects. He opposed promoting redevelopment for profit and prioritized finding sustainable solutions for urban aging problems through urban renewal and restoring community values. The only projects he pursued that were somewhat development-oriented were the makeover of the existing Gwanghwamun Square (광화문광장) and the Seoullo7017 (서울로7017) project that transformed a former highway overpass near Seoul Station into a plant-covered walkway. But they were, of course, redevelopment projects with sustainable solutions.

It would be incorrect to underestimate his policies and programs because they are not large-scale urban projects. Instead of seeking out marquee projects like Lee's Cheonggyecheon Restoration Project or Oh's Han River Renaissance Project, Park Won-soon took a more nuanced approach, enabling and cultivating Seoul's social capital with soft infrastructure like open data, urban regeneration support centers, and start-up incubators. He also didn't hesitate to carry out the unfinished projects started by the former mayor Oh Se-hoon. Park took over and successfully implemented Oh Se-hoon's plans like the introduction of a bike-sharing service to Seoul and the development plan of Seoul Dullae-gil (서울둘레길), a 157 km-long scenic walk trail course surrounding the city. Today, public bikes and Seoul Dullae-gil are two of the most popular urban programs among Seoul citizens. In the next three chapters, we will show how Park Won-soon contributed to the development of Seoul as a global leader in smart city interventions and coordinated policy.

Chapter 11

Car-Sharing for Better Mobility

In the 2010s, the *sharing economy* was booming across the globe. Airbnb and Uber, both San Francisco-based startups and pioneers of the sharing economy, soon became global unicorns. Their valuations reached over one billion dollars because of public acceptance of sharing options that could be easily accessed from smart phones and the lack of regulation of the sharing economy in its first years of development. Airbnb disrupted the global hospitality market by surpassing the 100-year-old hotel brand Hilton in just eight years, without the need of owning a single property. Hilton had been a star of the classical model of hospitality but did have the high overhead costs of property acquisition, development and staffing that took 93 years to secure 721,000 rooms in 88 countries. Comparatively, in their first 10 years of operation, Airbnb managed over six million property listings in 900 cities around the world. Uber, a ridesharing service startup founded in 2009 that allowed private citizens using private vehicles to join their company as drivers to pick up extra cash, followed a similar path, and the company became a unicorn in 2013. These companies ushered in a new model of business that was based on a well-organized platform on which private citizens could take an active role as providers of services, keeping fixed business costs low. The tremendous success of Uber and Airbnb sparked global interest in the sharing economy. The sharing economy has become a fixture of urban life and is an important area of the local economy that any county or city should not overlook, as its global market size is expected to skyrocket from US$15 billion in 2013 to US$335 billion in 2025. However, South Korea was only at the beginning stage of the sharing economy around 2010. Startups like Co-up (office sharing), Kiple (children's clothing sharing), and BnB Hero (room sharing) were beginning to appear, but evidence of the global sharing economy boom wasn't significant in South Korea.

Ironically, Korea is a nation with a strong cultural sense of sharing and the term 'Woori' (우리), roughly translated to westerners as 'The We,' is a national characteristic of the Korean people. Historically, Korea has been an agricultural producer, and even now the sharing of the labor force and resources like seeds, agricultural tools, and equipment is very common. The government also launched a ride-sharing campaign in the 1990s to encourage co-workers and residents with similar destinations to carpool to alleviate traffic congestion, and more than 25,000 people participated in the campaign. Unfortunately, the policy faded after 2–3 years due to the government's insufficient follow-up interventions.

The power of 'We' also proved to be pivotal in dealing with the 1997 IMF crisis in Korea. With the struggles of the postwar years still a vivid memory for most of the adult population, people took the recovery efforts seriously and banded together to share resources. This 'We' mentality was also apparent in the national gold campaign, in which the government requested that people donate their gold to pay back the IMF bailout loan. The result of this campaign was the collection of 225 tons of gold, worth about US$ 2.17 billion, which enabled South Korea to repay the IMF bailout loan *ahead* of schedule. The global media covered this campaign extensively because bailout loans often go into default, and the newly developed Korean economy was still untested as a global reference. The nationwide effort not only brought about the elimination of the IMF debt but also solidified the reputation of South Korea as a developed economy. Despite these successes, the sense of 'We' in Korea continued to be a part of the survival mentality that would be brought to the forefront only during difficult times, not a desirable practice to be used in times of prosperity. As the IMF crisis faded away and the Korean economy began to grow again, the sharing ecosystem was weaker than other countries at the time.

As sharing options became fashionable and the commercial success of sharing unicorns created hype, cities around the world were faced with the task of creating policies around this new economic force and Seoul was no exception. Mayor Park Won-soon, a natural ally of the sharing economy, announced the *Sharing Seoul Initiative* in 2012, right after he took office in October 2011. He considered individualism as a root-cause of urban problems and a barrier to fostering inclusive and sustainable growth. He had noticed the disappearing sense of community in Seoul and felt that as the city grew and modernized, people's feeling of individualism had intensified. A heightened sense of individualism increases congestion levels because of an increase in single occupancy vehicles on roads, potentially compounding urban problems like traffic jams, pollution, and parking shortages. Korean households had traditionally been multi-person (and multi-generational) spaces where resources were shared. With the trend toward individualism, resources meant for multiple people were being under-used and thrown away before the end of their lifespan, resulting in higher levels of waste. Park Won-soon believed the recovery of a sense of community to be an essential factor in resolving Seoul's urban problems. To address these concerns, the initiative introduced infrastructure to promote resource-sharing among Seoulites and encouraged the private sector to explore business models related to the sharing economy. Mayor Park Won-soon declared that he would solve the social and economic problems in Seoul by restoring the traditional sharing culture that had been lost due to urbanization. By establishing a system for the sharing of information and space, he looked to restore community ties, maximize resource utilization, and revitalize the urban economy. Shortly after the launch of this program, the sharing promotion ordinance was enacted to promote sharing services in both the private and public sectors.

Seoul Bike Ddareungi
(Source: Seoul Metropolitan Government)

With the deployment of Ddareungi, the number of
bicycle users in Seoul has increased significantly.

Under the Sharing Seoul Initiative, the Seoul Metropolitan Government opened meeting rooms and event halls in almost 800 government buildings to the public for business meetings or events and private gatherings. Mayor Park Won-soon also took over the bike-sharing project that Mayor Oh had started and expanded it throughout Seoul. Oh Se-hoon learned about North America's first large-scale bike sharing system 'BIXI Montréal' on a visit to Quebec, Canada and planned to introduce the service to Seoul in 2010. Unfortunately, Mayor Oh resigned before the project took shape. Under Mayor Park's leadership, Seoul's bike-sharing service was branded Ddareungi (따릉이) and grew into an essential public service for Seoul citizens. As of 2023, Seoul has a total length of about 940 km of bike paths, 37,500 units in operation, and one in three Seoul citizens is a registered 'Ddareungi' member.

The Park administration also introduced an online platform known as Sharehub (http://sharehub.kr), which served as a connection point for users to access sharing services and actively fostered a culture of sharing throughout the city. The Sharehub invited private companies and citizens to participate and supported over 50 sharing projects proposed by various stakeholders. This is how the Seoul government-led car-sharing service, the Nanumcar (나눔카) Project, was born in 2013.

The service concept of Nanumcar was to provide short-term car rentals that could be booked online by the minute, hour, or day. The car sharing service model itself is not a uniquely Korean idea, it has existed in many cities for years. The first car-sharing service is said to have been officially launched in Switzerland in 1948 as a service to those people who couldn't afford their own car. Since then, there have been a number of services to help people pool resources for better mobility options. During the following 50 years, similar small-scale car-sharing services were launched in communities in dense, global cities like Paris and Amsterdam. Zipcar was the first large-scale car-sharing company to come on the global scene in 2000. The use of the Internet, and later the smartphone, made this a viable business model that can be implemented on a national scale. Other car-sharing companies have also come on the scene with business models that allow for slightly different services, such as one-way car-sharing services and peer-to-peer rentals.

While car-sharing programs are relatively common, the Nanumcar program is unique from other car-sharing services that have popped up around the world. To begin with, the Nanumcar service runs on a public car-sharing platform. Most car-sharing companies have been private initiatives that required permission from local governments to function. Because mobility planning varies greatly, car-sharing options were often poorly integrated into the modal mix. Nanumcar was created, funded and managed by the Seoul Metropolitan Government, and the city's leadership on the Nanumcar platform made it possible for Seoul to have a more integrated program. Car-sharing startups, such as SOCAR (쏘카) and Greencar (그린카), were invited to participate in the Nanum Car program as partners.

Nanumcar Poster
(Source: Seoul Transport Operation & Information Service)

The Nanumcar project, started in 2013, ended in 2023 as car-sharing services in South Korea grew and became popular.

Before the active support of the Park administration, car-sharing startups were reluctant to enter the Seoul market. South Korea's car-sharing startups had launched their services in rural areas or tourism destinations like Jeju Island (제주도), South Korea's largest island and a popular tourist destination, where public transportation infrastructure was relatively poor. Part of the problem was parking fees and the scarcity of parking spaces available. The car-sharing business model is structured to enable users to pick up or return a car at designated parking lots. For start-ups, the availability of parking spaces in diverse and easily accessible locations is crucial, making parking fees a significant factor in the car-sharing model. Land prices in Seoul were over 20 times higher than those in other regions, so finding and leasing parking spots that would support a profit model was a nearly impossible task. Another reason why Korean car-sharing start-ups were reluctant to enter Seoul was because of the excellent public transportation system. As outlined in Chapter 4, the Seoul Public Transport Reform restructured transportation infrastructure in Seoul from vehicle-centered to people-oriented transport. By 2011, further improvements had been made to Seoul's public transport system. Although there was still significant usage of private transport options, public transport was prioritized in the city, and Seoul's modal share of public transportation had reached 74% in 2012, similar to or higher than in Tokyo (74.1%), Beijing (53.7%), and London (56.7%).

To ensure the success of the Nanumcar platform, Park Won-soon took an innovative approach to integrating these services into Seoul's transport network. First, the Park administration made public parking lots available to Korean car-sharing start-ups to encourage them to enter the market in Seoul. The Park Administration created *Nanumcar Parking Zones* in public parking lots with 10 or more spaces and leased parking spaces to the participating startups at a 50% discount. This intervention gave Korean ride-sharing startups the opportunity to launch in Seoul with confidence. Second, the Park administration incorporated these car sharing options into the T-money smart card payment platform, so that the same application that people use for public transportation could be used for car sharing. Park Won-soon's team realized that even with a stellar public transport system, there were still those who needed a car occasionally. Beyond the advantage of coordinated and regulated services with a common payment system, the Park administration also took steps to promote car-sharing by upgrading the fleet to electric vehicles in key areas and giving special incentives for car sharing to low-income and mobility-impaired groups. With the support given by the city government in parking allocation and inclusion in the mobility apps, these integrated car-sharing options targeted three types of usage:

a. Business – the Seoul government promoted car-sharing as a sustainable alternative to company cars. The providers offered robust business options like removal of unnecessary fixed costs (rental and parking fees), automatic fare collection of driving fees, and highway tolls.

b. Last mile for public transportation – car-sharing services were offered at some bus and train stations to allow commuters the option for last-mile car-sharing services when needed. A transfer discount was given to users who started a car-sharing trip at these stations within 30 minutes of exiting public transportation.

c. Residential – pre-booked car-sharing services for occasional use by the hour or by the day. This is commonly used as a more flexible alternative to traditional car rentals.

The Park administration had a good reason to promote car sharing in Seoul. Park Won-soon had set a goal of reducing greenhouse gas emissions by 40% by 2030, and reducing the number of cars on the road was an essential step to achieving this goal. Giving the people of Seoul pragmatic options to reduce their dependence on private vehicles would encourage the use of public transportation. This was a key intervention to make people rethink their need for private vehicles and increase the acceptance of sustainable transport policy in the city.

The launch of Nanumcar showed once again that what Seoul could do spectacularly well was mobility plan integration. While the Nanumcar program was active, an average of 912 people used it on a daily basis. In 2015, the Seoul Metropolitan Government surveyed 5,950 Nanumcar users and reported that the frequency of car use decreased by 36.3%, and the distance traveled by car decreased by 36.7% after using Nanumcar. The majority of respondents (62.2%) also answered that if the Nanumcar service continued, they would get rid of existing vehicles or not consider purchasing a private vehicle.

Without Mayor Park Won-soon's active policy support and mobility plan integration, it is doubtful that car-sharing companies would have set up and the momentum of mobility innovation could have been sustained in Seoul. The Park administration correctly identified an opportunity to boost sustainable transport policy with mobility options that complement the extensive metro and bus networks. In 2020, SOCAR became the first mobility Unicorn in South Korea and has an 80% share of the Korean car-sharing market. It operates more than 19,000 cars and 4,500 car-sharing zones in the Seoul Capital Area and has expanded to other Korean cities such as Daejeon (대전), Busan, Daegu and Gwangju (광주).

Park Won-soon was responsible for sparking South Korea's sharing economy and initiating a cultural change toward community-based solutions. He was also a pioneer in seeing the potential of partnering with the private sector to develop sustainable solutions for equitable transport in Seoul. His integrated model has successfully been extended to other cities in South Korea and has the potential to help other global cities solve their congestion and pollution problems to create a better quality of life for residents.

Key Takeaways:

- *Nanumcar is a public platform, which means that it is open to all car-sharing companies, not just a select few. By subsidizing parking, the program enabled car-sharing companies to enter the Seoul market.*

- *Nanumcar is integrated with the Seoul T-money platform, meaning people can easily use Nanumcar to get to and from public transportation hubs. This makes it a convenient option for people who may be able to live without a personal vehicle of their own.*

- *Nanumcar has been a success since its launch. In 2019, it had over 1 million registered users and over 3 million rides. The service has been praised for its convenience and affordability.*

Chapter 12

Enabling Data-Driven Urban Administration

A city, especially a global mega-city, is a factory for producing massive amounts of data. All types of data related to city administration, such as citizens' birth and death information, moving in and out dates, and individual tax reports, are recorded on a regular basis. Documentation related to policy and managerial decisions like urban master plans and investigation or progress reports are kept for years. Around 2010, it was not unusual to find city administration offices filled with stacks of documents and city staff spent hours of their day accessing data through complex filing systems, trying to make sense of the data. With the introduction of smart cities, the situation has worsened as data production in cities has exploded. CCTVs, installed across the city, transmit real-time video streams, and IoT sensors collect real-time city environment data such as temperature, humidity, dust levels, traffic congestion and floating population. As cities get smarter and more sensor technology is implemented for advancements such as autonomous vehicles, the speed of data production in cities is expected to expand even further.

For a long time, a gap existed between the collection of data and the meaningful use of data for decision-making. Many cities struggled with making sense of the collected data and using it to improve the city environment. Early on, it was not uncommon to find city data stored and managed in an isolated system that inhibited access by the broader governmental and non-governmental community. Data formats (JSON, text, etc.) and data storage products or solutions (Oracle DB, Hadoop, etc.) were not standardized, and data management teams varied across geographies.

In recent years, global cities have been making progress in gathering, analyzing and even opening data. The application area of city data is expanding and is used to improve decision-making in city administration in areas like crowd control, police patrol deployment, and bus route optimization. To promote data-driven city management, governments have begun launching new programs, such as the European Union's *open-source* data platform called 'FIWARE (www.fiware.org).' FIWARE was created in 2012 to encourage European cities to develop data-driven city management policies and smarter solutions, and it has helped an increasing number of cities to explore ways to use collected city data with less investment burden.

The city of Seoul is also leading the way in developing a pragmatic approach to using city data with the development of The *Digital Mayor's Office* (디지털시장실), an integrated smart city platform for data-driven urban administration. The Digital Mayor's Office is a three-meter-wide smart board that can be manipulated through a touch screen or voice/motion activation by the Mayor of Seoul. By looking at the smart board, the Mayor of Seoul can grasp the city's real-time status through a number of indicators such as revenue spending, number of daily accidents, citywide air pollution, traffic condition maps, and inflation rates. The mayor can also watch real-time news and social media updates with 'Seoul' as a key topic and even respond to urgent situations with work groups on-site through video conference meetings that allow him a 360-degree view of the issues while the meeting is in progress.

Digital Mayor's Office at CES 2020
(Source: Seoul Metropolitan Government)

Mayor Park Won-soon introduced and demonstrated the
Digital Mayor's Office at the Consumer Electronics Show (CES) in
Las Vegas, Nevada in 2020.

The Digital Mayor's Office project was launched in 2016, five years after Park Won-soon's inauguration. This was a high-profile project that was supervised directly by the mayor and which included the task of developing a comprehensive smart city platform connecting and incorporating 328 city systems and over 142 million data categories. These data categories included city infrastructure systems, such as approx. 60,000 CCTV cameras, Seoul's traffic control center, as well as administration systems such as civic complaint consultation systems and city statistical systems. Beyond the pressure of having to deal directly with the Mayor as the only 'customer,' the leader of the project would also have to organize and digitize the overflowing piles of documents in the Mayor's office, an arduous task for anyone. Mayor Park was insistent about developing this project because he believed in the power of this tool to make public decision-making more transparent. After five years of searching for the right person, Cho Yong-hyun took over the leadership of the project as Seoul's Big Data Officer.

Finally, the project got underway in June 2016. Despite some concern about readiness, the service launched in 2017, and the Digital Mayor's Office immediately became an essential tool for the mayor's daily work. The tool enabled the mayor to work more efficiently with a wealth of relevant data visible in a single dashboard, such as work reporting, decision-making, and emergency response. The project cost was around 600 million KRW (about US $450,000), including software development, system design and the purchase and installation of high-tech equipment such as a large touch screen, a motion detector, and an AI speaker. The project went more smoothly than expected. Worries turned out to be in vain that the greatest challenge would be integrating more than 300 city administration systems on such a limited budget in a short timeframe. Coordination of data disclosure among departments proceeded smoothly. There was no need to build and maintain a separate big data storage. According to Cho, the most difficult part was conducting the user interview.

"Interviewing Mayor Park was as difficult as picking a star in the night sky," he recalled. "The task force was only able to have one interview before the Digital Mayor's Office was completed. I had no choice but to follow Mayor Park around like a shadow, recording what the mayor was doing and documenting what the mayor saw."

This project has not only enabled the mayor and his staff to access city records quickly and easily but also enabled them to coordinate the information across several agencies so that they could get a comprehensive picture of events in the city at any given time. It is the first ever integrated data dashboard for the city of Seoul.

The development of the Digital Mayor's Office took about twelve months. The successful opening of this complex platform in such a short period of time was largely due to the fact that Seoul already had a digitally advanced administration environment at the time of implementation. To begin with, most information in Seoul was already digitized. South Korea was one of the most advanced countries in the world in e-government practices. Seoul had begun to implement the use of electronic records in the 1990s. The use of electronic documents had been finetuned over the years and was already quite sophisticated by the time the Digital Mayor's Office project was developed. In addition to having digitized records, leadership for Seoul's e-government policies was strong. The first Chief Information Officer (CIO) of Seoul was appointed in 1999, making it one of the first global cities to focus on data. Because the position was established so early, the CIO had a more defined role in city government and had become an integral part of Seoul's administrative system. Under the CIO's leadership, Seoul had developed mid-to-long-term integrated e-government master plans with tasks aligned across government offices rather than working in silos on one-off projects.

Also, Seoul already had experience in city data integration. In 2005, the city of Seoul had launched a website that unified 126 websites run by different departments or affiliated organizations into a single integrated portal. The website (https://www.seoul.go.kr) not only provides news and policy updates from city authorities but also serves as a portal for over 680 types of civil petitions, such as certificate applications and museum reservations.

Another factor was that open data culture already existed in Seoul. The Park administration launched a data portal called Open Data Plaza (열린데이터광장) in 2012, aiming to provide the general public with city data. As of 2023, the website (https://data.seoul.go.kr) publishes about 7,000 types of public data, and more than 5,000 datasets are provided in the form of an open API (Application Program Interface). Private companies can leverage open data for data-driven services, such as providing real-time bus arrival information, weather updates, emergency alerts, and accident location data. Because open data culture had already been established, Seoul had high-quality urban data infrastructure in place by the time the Digital Mayor's Office was developed. This condition gave the project team a head start in building a more advanced smart city tool. Seoul's existing data infrastructure, including information digitalization, data standardization, big data platform development, and coordination between departments and stakeholders for system interfacing, allowed for the rapid development of the Digital Mayor's Office.

"Seoul was a pioneer in open data policies," explained Dr. Hwang Jong-sung, who served as CIO under Park Won-soon from 2011 to 2013 and is currently the President of the National Information Society Agency, the national agency that creates data strategy for South Korea.

"Seoul launched the open government portal (https://open gov.seoul.go.kr) in 2012 when it became clear that there was a demand for this. The portal opened administrative documents and records of the Seoul government to the citizens of Seoul. This meant that for any decision that was made on the city level, except for a few top-secret actions, there was a public record of who approved the decision, as well as a list of advisory members and the budget execution details. Of course, there was a lot of resistance to this open data policy internally, but we felt that it was important because even if few people accessed this information, this increased the level of transparency and created more trust in the government."

Park Won-soon went to step further. He wanted fully transparent systems for a better informed and empowered population and pursued real-time disclosure of information on municipal affairs to citizens. After establishing the Digital Mayor's Office for government, he extended the project to public access with the launch of the mobile version of the Digital Mayor's Office and the installation of the Digital Mayor's Office smart boards in public spaces like subway stations.

What really made the Digital Mayor's Office a paradigm-shifting policy was that the administration of Park Won-soon opened all of the past and present data to the public. This was not just open data like we see in so many other cities around the world; it was *digital transparency* that allowed the public the same access (with a few exceptions based on security issues) as high-level city officials. The introduction of a digital database that includes real-time data as well as stores of older data has transformed the way citizens of Seoul think about their government as well as the way government officials think about themselves.

**Mobile Version of Digital Mayor's Office (left) and
the Board installed at Subway Station (right)**
(Source: Seoul Metropolitan Government)

It could be said that the Digital Mayor's Office functioned as a panopticon of Seoul. The term panopticon is a philosophical concept meaning 'all-seeing' that was coined by Michel Foucault and refers to a phenomenon in which people will self-regulate when there is a possibility that they are being watched. Mayor Park Won-soon monitored the progress of Seoul's ongoing programs and policies through information displayed on the Digital Mayor's Office, which he always had access to in real-time. When the tool became available to the citizens of Seoul, citizens also had the ability to monitor Mayor

Park's performance on his policy promises in real-time. That is to say, the Digital Mayor's Office completed a virtuous circle in which there was greater transparency for Seoulites into Mayor Park's activities and for Mayor Park into the performance of Seoul city government programs.

This advanced open data policy with the Digital Mayor's Office tool has had a profound effect on the way that the city functions and has set the scene for continued growth and development in three ways:

1. **It increased trust in the government.** Korean society still has strong Confucian undertones that were cultivated during the 500 years of the Joseon dynasty. One of the basic principles of Confucianism is abiding by a social hierarchy that gives respect to elders and people in higher positions. It could be argued that in the modern era, this focus on hierarchy has given way to corruption due to the unquestioning respect given to those in the upper ranks of the social hierarchy. Open data and transparency is the enemy of corruption as it exposes unjust actions and incriminates those who undertake them. By opening up all data in the city, including the system of approvals for all expenditures, the Park Administration took a step toward making city finances and administration more transparent. The fact that all of these approvals and transactions are now kept on public record so that anyone can see them at any time makes public officials more accountable to the government and their constituency. In the end, the number of private citizens that will investigate possible corruption is extremely few, but the fact that they may do so whenever they choose makes public officials more compliant with anti-corruption policies and

also makes private citizens have more trust in their local government.

2. **It promotes entrepreneurship and innovation.** Open data policies worldwide are created to build higher levels of public engagement. In New York City, data sets have been made accessible to the public by the Mayor's Office of Data Analytics in an effort to promote both social and urban entrepreneurship. They are simple data sets, raw data that the city government allows people to access in the hopes that this data will enable the creation of technological tools for social issues and business models for an urban setting. Seoul's Digital Mayor's Office goes one step further by making sense of the data and showing how it fits into the city setting. This information serves as inspiration to entrepreneurs to identify areas ripe for innovation, where they can develop their vision for next-generation projects.

3. **It has made Seoul a leader in the 4th Industrial Revolution.** The story of smart city building in Seoul is not only about developing tools to enhance equity and the quality of life of the people of Seoul, but also about taking leadership in the development of a new urban model. The use of big data in creating a transparent society with efficient use of resources is one of the greatest challenges of the 4th Industrial Revolution, and the Digital Mayor's Office has created a roadmap for how cities can do this. This development and the knowledge-sharing activity associated with it has enabled other cities around the region and the globe to create and advance their big data policies using the best practices from Seoul.

Open data can be powerful. It has huge potential to impact the way that communities live and interact with each other. Park Won-soon often used the analogy that if a fire broke out, citizens could find a way to avoid the incident if they had access to the right information in a timely manner. Even if the Seoul Metropolitan Government struggled to come up with emergency response measures, transparent information could save citizens' lives by helping them find ways to avoid or overcome the situation.

When Park Won-soon talked about a fire breaking out, he probably imagined a situation like the Itaewon Tragedy of 2022. On Halloween in 2022, 159 people died in the area of Itaewon in Central Seoul because of a crowd surge. Itaewon is a popular area of central Seoul with a vibrant nightlife. Over the years it has become *the* location for Halloween festivities in South Korea, with people traveling from around the country to celebrate on October 31st, 2022. This was the first Halloween after the COVID-19 lockdowns, and over 130,000 people flocked to Itaewon. Although large crowds were expected, the district and public officials in charge missed the warning signs and did not make necessary preparations for crowd control, resulting in tragedy.

Seoul is arguably one of the most progressive cities in the world in terms of data-based processes. CCTVs are installed everywhere, including Itaewon, and transfer real-time street scenes to Seoul's centralized surveillance center. Cell towers in central Seoul are among the most efficient in the world in using cell signals to measure crowd density. Social media chatter leading up to that evening indicated crowds would be big. Seoul's modern subway system is equipped with advanced technology to measure the size of crowds by weight of the subway cars in real-time. Dozens of calls were placed to the local police station about the same street in the hours leading up to the tragedy. Lack of data was not the issue.

It turns out that open data is not enough. Data-based

decision-making involves a team of analysts and policymakers to decipher the raw data, but the public is generally not able to analyze data. Making public data an effective tool for public information and emergency response systems requires *process* and *design*.

A process could have been implemented to listen to social media chatter and create a crowd control plan when chatter reaches a certain level. CCTV and cell tower sensors to measure crowd density could be programmed to sound alarms that go directly to emergency care services when they rise above a certain threshold. The cell density sensors could also trigger an automatic push notification to cell users in the immediate vicinity, informing them of dangerous density levels and encouraging them to clear the area or stay away. Also, the weight sensors in the metro system could trigger an automatic shutdown of a metro stop to ease the flow of traffic into a congested area. And calls to the police in the hours leading up to the tragedy were answered by live officers, so they could have a mechanism in place to log calls with keyword recognition that then indicates a threat level to on-duty officers. One of the most heart-wrenching videos that circulated of the tragedy was of a police officer who happened upon the area after responding to a separate call nearby. He was desperately trying to steer people away from the alleyway but didn't have the tools to make people understand the gravity of his warnings, especially with the diluted authority of his police uniform on Halloween.

The Itaewon case is the worst of a series of crowd surge tragedies that have occurred in recent years, including cases in the United States and Indonesia, and highlights the importance of data process and design in emergency response situations. The data was available, but the procedures had not yet evolved enough to make the information effective in such dynamically changing conditions. As data policy is expanded in Seoul and South Korea, data-driven tools such as the Digital

Mayor's Office will certainly be developed with the weight of this event in mind.

"The use of data is constantly evolving and changing. There is enormous potential for data-based tools to improve the way the city functions. We have been developing better designs for data-based policy, but the Itaewon tragedy has pushed us to work harder and smarter," says Dr. Hwang. "The 159 young lives lost in Itaewon weighs on us as we know we can ensure this never happens again. For this reason, we are trying to develop data infrastructure to prioritize the process and design of public data in Seoul and throughout the country. We can't bring those young people back, but we can take inspiration from them to be better as a government and as a nation."

> ### Key Takeaways:
>
> - *Park Won-soon created the Digital Mayor's Office, a powerful tool that allows the Mayor of Seoul to grasp the city's real-time status through a number of indicators. This information can be used to make informed decisions about a wide range of issues, such as resource allocation, public safety, and transportation planning.*
>
> - *The Digital Mayor's Office was developed in a relatively short period of time due to Seoul's already digitized records and strong leadership for e-government policies. This allowed the project team to focus on integrating data from different city systems and developing a user-friendly interface.*
>
> - *Other cities can learn from the Digital Mayor's Office to create a valuable tool to improve their data-driven decision-making processes. By making city data available to the public, cities can encourage innovation and improve the quality of life for their residents.*

Chapter 13

Taking the Seoul Model Global

In East Asian mythology, there is a story about the founding of Korea. Like Zeus in Greek mythology, there was a god of the sky. He had a son who liked the earth very much and wanted to come down to earth to live among the mountains and the forests. The father looked all over the earth and determined that the Korean Peninsula would be the place where the philosophy of *Hongik-Ingan* (홍익인간), roughly translated as 'broadly benefitting the human world,' might flourish. This philosophy has a strong element of compassion and interconnectedness that has been incorporated into Korean culture for centuries. Hongik-Ingan became the official motto of the South Korean education system in the post-war constitution of 1948, and Koreans have grown up learning that their responsibility is to 'broadly benefit the human world.'

Considering South Korea's miraculous economic growth in a short period, it is understandable that Korea was too busy surviving to benefit humanity in the first few decades after the constitution was written. The people of Korea had to focus on their immediate environment to escape poverty and rebuild after the destruction of the Korean War. But the lessons of Hongik-Ingan stayed with them spiritually and, as the country developed, a sense of interconnectedness with the world was always part of their thought process. This may be why Koreans place such an unusually high level of importance on knowledge sharing and benchmarking when traveling to other cities.

In 1996, South Korea joined the OECD and adopted the mission to promote policies that would improve the economic and social well-being of people around the world. This served as a turning point for the way in which South Korea interacted with the global community and kick-started a new phase of history in which South Korea played the role of mentor to other countries.

This book has given an overview of the major projects that the three mayors have implemented to drastically improve the urban environment in Seoul. These services have had a profound effect on the quality of life of Seoulites by improving their environment as well as their access to socioeconomic opportunities. The policies enacted by the government have worked to broadly benefit the local community, so it was a natural step for them to consider how they can extend the reach of these benefits to the rest of the world.

When it comes to piloting and diffusing innovative city services for the improvement of the citizen experience, Seoul has taken a leadership role. Mayor Lee Myung-bak's Cheonggyecheon Restoration Project unleashed an emphasis on nature-based solutions in Korean cities, and his public transport reforms continue to inspire a multitude of public transport projects across South Korea and beyond. Following the success of Lee Myung-bak's interventions, new cities or towns built in South Korea often include a large-scale lake park and BRT lines starting in the design stage. The city of Sejong (세종시), a brand-new town where most national government agencies are located, is a good example. Sejong was established in 2012 as the administrative capital of South Korea, similar to Brasilia or Canberra. Sejong City is famous for its BRT line, as well as the rivers and tributaries that form waterside walks and bike routes throughout the city center. Mayor Oh Se-hoon's public design guidelines for Seoul brought the idea of public sector design to the fore-front of urban development practices. Following Seoul's example, more than 60 Korean cities have established their own public space and utility design guidelines, and this has contributed to the beautification of major cities in South Korea. Park Won-soon's pioneering open data policy was also later adopted by South Korea's Ministry of the Interior and Safety (MOIS) with the Public Data Act, which framed an open data policy for the entire nation. The Act led to the launch and operation of the open data portal (https://www.data.go.kr/), accessible or down-loadable not only to citizens and companies in Korea but also to overseas researchers or companies. The scope of open data includes, but is not limited to, real-time IoT sensor collection data such as temperature and humidity, national or local statistics, administrative documents, and historical photo records. Most of the photos included in this book were sourced from data released by Seoul and the Korean government.

The benchmarking of Seoul's best practices is, of course, not limited to local governments in Korea. Every year, many national and local governments from other parts of the world visit South Korea to benchmark their innovative services. Since Lee Myung-bak launched the Cheonggyecheon Restoration Project and implemented the Seoul Public Transport Reform, the world has taken notice and the number of foreign institutions, public agencies, and multinational organizations visiting Seoul to benchmark Seoul's smart city interventions has been on the rise. Nearly 2,500 key figures from 19 foreign governments came to see Cheonggyecheon in the first two years. During Mayor Oh Se-hoon's first term, 50 countries and 800 municipalities and organizations visited Seoul to bench-mark the 120 Dasan Seoul program, a centralized hotline for city services created to streamline communication with residents, tourists, and the underprivileged. By 2013, Mayor Park Won-soon welcomed 6,213 foreign government officials for knowledge-sharing on Korea's best practices in smart and sustainable developments. The mayors of San Francisco, Amsterdam and Mecca, in addition to Ministers of Transportation and other high-level city officials, all came to Seoul to study urban interventions and share best practices that year.

However, there are limits to the effectiveness of benchmarking. Many of the benchmarking visits to Seoul showed great potential, but fizzled out after the delegates returned to their home countries. Global cities have different resources, budget priorities and political landscapes. While 5G networks are ubiquitously deployed throughout Seoul, there are countries in the world that have yet to launch 4G (LTE) service. Even though foreign city officials may have learned best practices from Seoul officials, that doesn't mean they could easily make changes in their home cities. Overall, local governments in other parts of the world had difficulties importing Seoul's advanced technologies and policies because of limits on financial resources and technical capabilities. As a result, site visits for benchmarking often ended without specific results or action items. While the Seoul government is happy to host foreign governments to improve bilateral relations, there was a feeling that they could do more to foster smart solutions worldwide.

Seoul has built global leadership in a relatively short period of time, so smart city best practices from Seoul are especially interesting for cities in development that hope to emulate Seoul's rapid transformation. In 2008, Oh Se-hoon hosted the World e-Government Mayors Forum in Seoul and used the opportunity with the mayors in attendance to introduce the idea of a global network for local governments. As a result of this meeting, the World e-Government Organizations for Cities and Local Governments (https://we-gov.org/), or WeGO, was founded in 2010 as a membership-based international association of local governments. The association started with 50 member cities and has grown into a large-scale international organization with 215 members, including 160 local government members, 37 corporations, and 18 institutions.

Park Won-soon shared Oh Se-hoon's vision for Seoul's global leadership in the transformation of world cities into smart cities and established the Seoul Urban Solutions Agency (서울시정책수출사업단), or SUSA, in 2015. SUSA's objective is to share Seoul's expertise and know-how in smart city development to contribute to the creation of sustainable urban communities around the globe. Since its establishment, SUSA has consulted on project developments in global cities interested in importing Seoul's smart city expertise.

SUSA's brochure underlines the mentality of Hongik-Ingan, stating that "Seoul rose to a world-class city with the development support of the global community. By sharing our growth experience, Seoul can provide support in improving urban livelihood for other cities to grow into smart, livable, environmentally and economically sustainable urban domains."

SUSA undertakes a variety of activities, including knowledge sharing, training, project funding, and project delivery in a variety of sectors where Seoul has a wealth of experience.

1. Public Transportation – covering the Seoul Public Transport Reform and upgrades to the bus fleet and intelligent transport management systems that have taken place since.

2. Waste Management – covering Seoul's resource-recycling city model to reduce waste and raise the recycling rate through a public-private partnership approach.

3. Water Management – branding Seoul's clean tap water from the Han River under the name Arisu (아리수) and sharing knowledge on the management skills of water sources, purification technologies, and sewage treatment practices to cities in developing countries like Arusha in Tanzania, Hai Duong in Vietnam and Pulau Muara Besar in Brunei.

4. Housing Solutions – providing consultation on public housing policies to relieve housing shortages and to address issues of affordable housing and structural changes in housing markets.

5. Nature-based Solutions – transferring the know-how of the Cheonggyecheon Restoration model on how to bring greenspace and natural ecosystems back to the urban environment to local governments in overseas cities in the United States and Vietnam.

6. e-Government Systems – leveraging Seoul's experience in developing and managing e-government public service, administration systems and advanced big data practices to improve communications between citizens and the government. Ranked #1 in the UN e-government survey for 5 years straight, Seoul has funded overseas e-government development projects since 2016. Kampala's civic service system and Bandung's tax information system are a few examples of these projects.

7. Emergency Response – Opening details of K-quarantine, which effectively mitigated the spread of COVID-19 in its early stages, and became known globally as 3T (Test, Tracing, Treatment). SUSA proactively assisted benchmarking visits for global cities and international institutions like the United Nations and World Health Organization.

As a result of Korea's focus on international cooperation, the influence of Seoul's smart services on local development has been felt in many cities worldwide. A particularly notable achievement is the global export of Seoul's smart public transportation services. Baku, the capital of Azerbaijan, has imported Seoul's intelligent transport systems (ITS) best practices. Major city roads in Baku have CCTVs for real-time monitoring of traffic conditions, and bus stations in the city provide bus departure and arrival times through the bus information system (BIS). The city also has its own Transport Operation & Information Service (TOPIS) Center that gathers and processes real-time traffic and transport information to enable the city to manage road and subway train traffic efficiently. Korean companies played an integral role in facilitating Baku's transformation of public transport infrastructure.

Seoul's smart card service was also exported to New Zealand and Malaysia, where it brought about a reduction in traffic congestion and an increase in the use of public transportation in both cities. Perhaps most significantly, Seoul transitioned from an importer to exporter of transport best practices in Bogota. The Seoul government visited Bogota, Colombia, for BRT bus system benchmarking in 2002 to learn BRT best practices from the Colombian authorities and then returned the favor in 2011 to share knowledge about advanced smart card systems for service upgrades in public transportation systems with Bogota's transport authorities. There are many more cases in which Seoul played an active role in exporting their knowledge for global development projects, such as policy creation for Intelligent Transport Systems in Mongolia, advising on data-based public transport upgrades in Ukraine and the implementation of Intelligent Transport Systems in Kenya.

Besides exporting Seoul's proven smart city services in partnership with Korean companies, the city of Seoul with SUSA has made multifaceted efforts to enable and strengthen smart city policy capabilities of overseas cities. Under the leadership of Mayor Park, the Seoul Metropolitan Government once operated a program that invited 18 public officials from 10 WeGO member cities and shared professional and technical knowledge on Seoul's e-government and smart services for eight days in 2013. This program was incorporated into one of SUSA's main tasks, and public officials from countries like India and El Salvador could gain a more detailed understanding of how Seoul successfully implemented key smart city programs. Alongside various professionals and experts in Seoul's urban policy and smart city fields, SUSA has also served as a consultant for overseas cities by establishing smart city master plans or conducting feasibility studies or surveys. Many overseas cities have been the beneficiary of SUSA projects, such as Buenos Aires, Kampala, Kyiv, and Ulaanbaatar.

Mayor Park Won-soon did not stop there. He became a global PR ambassador for Seoul Smart City. Not only did he personally give a keynote speech on Seoul's smart city at CES, the world's largest ICT fair held annually in Las Vegas, in 2020, but he also took part in a demonstration of the Digital Mayor's Office outside of Seoul City Hall imploring attendees to "refer to Seoul if you dream of a smart city."

All in all, Mayor Park Won-soon's leadership and knowledge-sharing initiative leveraged the national consciousness and revived the Hongik Ingan ideology for the development of SUSA. This development serves as an essential vehicle for sharing Seoul's knowledge and experience globally to broadly benefit the human world.

Key Takeaways:

- *After benefiting from international collaboration in the post-war period, Park Won-soon's government was keen to give back and raise the profile of Seoul's smart city policies. This has been a driving force behind the city's efforts to share its knowledge and experience with other cities.*

- *The World e-Government Organizations for Cities and Local Governments (WeGO) and the Seoul Urban Solutions Agency (SUSA) are two organizations that have played a key role in helping Seoul to share its smart city expertise with other cities.*

- *Seoul's smart city expertise has been used in a number of cities around the world, including cities across east and central Asia, as well as Latin America.*

2020 and BEYOND

The Seoul Landscape by Lina Lee

The Return of Oh Se-hoon

Oh Se-hoon became the Mayor of Seoul again in 2021. In mid-2020, tragedy struck Seoul when Mayor Park Won-soon committed suicide after receiving the news that his secretary had accused him of sexual harassment. The news shocked the nation and the world in part because Park Won-soon had been a lifelong defender of women's rights and had even proclaimed himself a 'feminist' in a country where the term has a derogatory connotation. He had also been a favorite to become the next president of South Korea after Moon Jae-in's term ended in 2022. After Park Won-soon's death, the city of Seoul functioned without a mayor for over nine months until Oh Se-hoon was chosen to fill the vacant seat in a by-election in April 2021. A year later, Mayor Oh Se-hoon was re-elected for a full-term in Seoul's 8th mayoral election. This victory gave him the distinction of being the first person to be elected Mayor on four different occasions by the people of Seoul.

When he began his full-term later that year, Oh Se-hoon announced his blueprint for Seoul for the next decade, his *Seoul Vision 2030*. Part of his campaign promise had been to build a robust mechanism for public consultation on his plan for the city, and he kept that promise. Through a committee composed of 44 experts and 78 citizens selected from various fields and all levels of society, the Seoul Vision 2030 master plan was finalized after more than 100 public debates during the first 136 days of Oh Se-hoon's third mayoral term and set

78 policy tasks essential to realize its vision. Some of the most prominent points of his plan include:

1. **Han River Renaissance Project 2.0** – Under Mayor Oh's leadership, the role of the Han River will be expanded to a global tourist destination that provides a variety of things to enjoy. The Project, also known as 'The Great Han River Project,' aligns with Mayor Oh's ambition to attract 30 million tourists annually. Before the COVID-19 pandemic, the number of overseas visitors to Seoul was about 14 million. The project includes the construction of the world's largest spokeless Ferris wheel, called 'Seoul Ring,' and tours of Seoul in flying cars (Urban Air Mobility).

2. **More Sustainable Waterfront Recreation Spaces** – Building on the success of the Han River Renaissance Project and the Cheonggyecheon Restoration Project, Oh Se-hoon is also contemplating a 'Local Stream Renaissance project.' Taking advantage of smaller streams throughout the city, the Seoul government is looking to create an urban recreational network where any citizen in Seoul can enjoy various outdoor activities in their communities like they do in the Han River area.

3. **Beauty Industry Hub** – DDP and the surrounding area will become a hub for the Korean beauty industry while concurrently strengthening their existing role as a hub for the Korean design industry. K-beauty has become a powerhouse industry in recent years and was valued at US$11.8 billion in 2022. Projections suggest that this growth will continue to make it a US$16.2 billion industry by 2028, and Oh Se-hoon sees the opportunity to augment this growth with a themed area of Seoul.

4. **Cultural and Art Landmark Space** – Oh Se-hoon is looking to continue Mayor Park Won-soon's efforts to make Gwanghwamun Square into a venue for art and culture. Gwanghwamun Square (광화문광장) is a public square with statues of two of Korea's greatest heroes: King Sejong (세종대왕), the inventor of Hangul, the Korean alphabet, and the Admiral Yi Sun-sin (이순신장군), who is famous for his strategic victories against a much larger Japanese navy during the Joseon Dynasty (which was depicted in the blockbuster film *The Admiral: Roaring Currents* from 2014). Gwanghwamun Square resembled an isolated island, difficult for citizens and tourists to access due to the main roads on both sides with a width exceeding 30 meters. The Square was remodeled and opened as Seoul's urban park in August 2022. As Seoul's cultural landmark space, Gwanghwamun Square has hosted various outdoor exhibitions and events, including moonlight yoga, outdoor concerts, movie nights, and summer festivals.

5. **Metaverse Seoul** – Oh Se-hoon declared that Seoul would be the first city in the Metaverse. He kept his promise as the city of Seoul launched 'Metaverse Seoul' in January 2023. Metaverse Seoul allows Seoul citizens to use avatars to explore a virtual Seoul City Hall, play games in Seoul Plaza (서울광장), and, most importantly, make consultations on public services. Metaverse Seoul earned the title of the world's first public service platform in Metaverse and is listed in Time magazine's 200 best inventions of 2022.

6. **Affordable Housing** – Not only is the city planning to add 80,000 units to housing stock annually, but

special attention will be given to the younger generation of professionals who are currently priced out of the market.

7. **Digital Citizen Mayor's Office** – Park Won-soon's signature project, which allowed the mayor a 360-degree view of government processes and helped build transparency in the city, will be upgraded to make it more widely accessible for Seoul's government officials.

8. **Global Leadership** – SUSA will continue to help Mayor Oh Se-hoon promote Seoul as a smart city capital by exporting the city's expertise worldwide to address urban problems and promote smart city policies that will improve people's economic and social well-being worldwide.

Oh Se-hoon has his work cut out for him with such an ambitious plan to propel Seoul into the next phase of urban development, but he is able to draw on his extensive experience in city government and two decades of consistent smart city and sustainability policy development in Seoul. The fact that he and his predecessors have focused on smart interventions has not only created a wealth of experience and knowledge in leadership in Seoul, but it has also created an empowered municipal government workforce that will enable him to implement these ambitious goals with greater agility.

Conclusion

The competition among world cities to occupy the position of the world's leading smart city is fierce. Barcelona has made itself synonymous with the words 'smart city' by hosting the annual global gathering for smart city development since 2011, the Smart City World Congress. Singapore has risen to international fame with its Smart Nation Initiative and the creation of a digital twin for the entire country. Paris came to fame in recent years with their '15-minute city' urban policy. Saudi Arabia has recently started building Neom, a greenfield US$500 billion futuristic mega city to be built in the desert with next-generation technology. There is no end to the list of cities looking to build their soft power quotient by launching headline-grabbing smart interventions.

As much as smart city development has started to enter the sphere of nation-building and international politics, the smart city movement is about people and quality of life. The onset of the digital age has allowed city governments to take advantage of technology to provide a more comprehensive set of tools for citizen engagement in a more transparent format. The story of Seoul's development into a smart city is significant because the city not only accomplished this task with exceptional efficiency, but it did so under the conditions of expansive growth.

As we observe the state of the world in 2023, we see cities in the developed and developing world struggling with urban revitalization after years of uncontrolled activity. Industrial centers, brought to cities at great expense for job creation initiatives, pollute and physically blight communities. Public transportation has been neglected and become unreliable and unsustainable in many urban centers, causing traffic to sky-rocket and air quality to plummet. Trust in government is at an all-time low, with few tools to bring transparency in public finances and decision-making. Climate change effects of commercial and industrial practices are taking their toll on cities and creating heat island and desertification effects in urban settings. These are all complaints that could have been made about Seoul in the year 2000, but because of the work of three mayoral administrations, Seoul has overcome these problems to create a better quality of life for residents.

Lee Myung-bak initiated the process of smart city development by making fundamental and inspiring changes to the city. He enabled greater freedom of movement for residents and gave them a little bit of breathing space in the dense urban fabric of the city. The raging bulldozer showed the world that dramatic changes could be implemented and was much lauded for his effectiveness.

Oh Se-hoon, in his first term, took over from Lee Myung-bak and continued efforts to make the city more livable with waterfront recreational space. He also added beautification efforts so that Seoul would match the style and elegance that Koreans had become known for globally, and he made efforts to ensure that all Seoulites were able to live comfortably.

Park Won-soon inherited a relatively smart city from Oh Se-hoon and sought to bring a greater sense of community to people's everyday lives. He reasoned that the sharing culture was a good fit with Korean values and that greater transparency with open data would help people believe in the democratic process and increase their interaction with the city. He also believed that it was time to give back to the global community that had helped Korea when the country was in need.

Now, Seoul is in the hands of Oh Se-hoon once again. This book closes by looking forward to seeing how Seoul will absorb the 4th Industrial Revolution technologies accelerated by the COVID-19 pandemic and what Seoul will look like in 2030. But Oh Se-hoon's outlook is different now. Thanks to the work done over the past 20 years, he is leading a global city with a well-known reputation for excellence in urban development.

Even with all of the success of the past 20 years, Seoul is not the perfect smart city or a perfect city. There is considerable work still to be done to bring greater equity and environmental sustainability for the future, but the transformation that Seoul has undergone from a problematic, overcrowded city to a smart, sustainable city is exceptional and can serve as a roadmap, or at least as inspiration, for cities across the world.

Urban development is like a work of art; the greatest achievements can't be replicated. Each new work has to express the vision of the artist and be adapted to the conditions the artist is working under. For this reason, we feel that smart city Seoul is the product of visionary policies implemented by the city's three mayors of the 21st century: Lee Myung-bak, Oh Se-hoon and Park Won-soon. Just like Francisco de Goya adapted his style and technique to each new work, so did Lee Myung-bak adapt what he had learned about urban development to best benefit the needs of Seoul. Oh Se-hoon adapted to the new reality of the city Lee Myung-bak had built, and then Park Won-soon adapted to Oh Se-soon's version of Seoul. It cannot be overstated how important continuity has been to the success of Seoul's Smart City Policy, with each mayor building on the work of the last. Smart city Seoul is a multi-generational work of art.

Appendix

GLOSSARY OF TERMS

AI

AI is the acronym for Artificial Intelligence and indicates the intelligence of machines and software that mimics human capability in problem-solving or performing tasks. AIs are generally used for automating business processes, gaining insight through data analysis, etc.

API

API stands for Application Programming Interface. API is a code or protocol that allows two or more computer programs to communicate with each other and assists in simplifying the integration of two or more applications or systems.

AR

The acronym for Augmented Reality and a technology that superimposes a computer-generated digital image on a user's view of the real world, thus providing a composite view.

Big Data

Refers to a set of large, complex, and hard-to-manage data. Big data is difficult to analyze with personal software such as Excel and requires more advanced and high-end computing functions and software optimized for big data.

Build-Operate-Transfer (BOT)
A project financing and development model used for large infrastructure and public-private partnership (PPP) projects. The primary motivation behind the BOT model is to leverage private sector expertise and financing to develop much-needed infrastructure without placing a heavy burden on public budgets. It allows governments to access private sector resources and skills to complete projects more efficiently and quickly.

Data-driven decision making
A decision-making approach that goes through the validation process to collect and interpret data and make decisions based on reliable data, insights, and facts.

Developmental Dictatorship
A system in which the economy was prioritized under the authorization leadership, the type of regime and development model that raised many parts of Asia out of abject poverty.

e-Government
Electronic or digital government using the internet, the world-wide-web or other information technologies to enhance the efficiency and effectiveness of service or information delivery in the public sector.

4th Industrial Revolution
The current and developing environment in which disruptive technologies such as Big Data, Artificial Intelligence, the Internet of Things, and 5G are changing the way modern people live and work. The term was coined in 2016 by Klaus Schwab, the founder of the World Economic Forum.

4G (LTE)   The fourth generation technology standard of broadband wireless cellular networks, also called Long Term Evolution. After 4G, users have become more comfortable watching real-stream videos or games on mobile phones.

5G   The fifth generation technology standard of broadband wireless cellular networks, which enables faster and more efficient connections and increased reliability, makes it easier to transfer high-resolution digital content like AR, real-stream or virtual reality games.

Hangul   The Korean alphabet is made up of 24 letters: 14 consonants and 10 vowels. Hangul was created in the mid-fifteenth century by King Sejong, a ruler in the Joseon Dynasty.

ICT   The concept of ICT is similar to or interchangeable with IT. However, ICT covers wired and wireless communication technologies as well as computing technologies like servers or software applications.

Internet of Things (IoT)   Physical objects with sensors that connect and exchange data with other devices and systems over the Internet.

IT   As the acronym of Information Technology, IT is a broad term that involves the use of computing technologies like servers, laptop computers, software applications and other digital or electronic means to communicate, transfer data and process information.

Joense   A unique housing rental agreement that only exists in South Korea, the tenant pays a large lump-sum deposit for the duration of the contract instead of monthly rent.

Korean Wave Also known as Hallyu, refers to a cultural phenomenon in which the global popularity of South Korea's cultural products like K-pop, movies, and TV dramas have dramatically risen since the early 2000s.

Metaverse A computer-generated virtual environment in which users can interact as avatars with each other, create and play games, work and shop.

Miracle on the Han River A nickname that symbolizes South Korea's fast post-war recovery and rapid economic growth in the 1970s and 1980s. South Korea earned this globally-known nickname after successfully hosting the 1988 Seoul Olympic Games.

Nature-based Solutions An urban planning intervention approach that regenerates areas affected by human activities and restores key ecological functions using natural features or processes.

Open data Refers to data that is openly accessible, exploitable, editable and shared by anyone for any purpose. Around 2012, the open data movement started, initially led by the United Kingdom and European Union. Today, many countries and institutions across the globe are implementing various programs or policies related to open data.

Seoulite Refers to any person of, from, or pertaining to Seoul, regardless of origin or documentation status.

Seoul Metropolitan Area

The metropolitan area of Seoul. The area geographically covers not only Seoul but also Incheon and Gyeonggi provinces. The area is composed of 28 cities and home to about half of the Korean population.

Sharing Economy

An economic model in which assets and services are shared between individuals or groups in a collaborative way. The model has been globally welcomed because of its multiple socio-economic benefits, such as providing more affordable and accessible options to everyone, allowing us to better protect our environment by reducing production, and making it easier for startups and aspiring entrepreneurs to launch their business ideas over the internet.

Smart Card

A physical plastic card with a micro processor or memory chip, similar to a credit card, to make cashless payments or for convenience of any transaction.

Smart City

A city that uses IT or ICT to solve urban problems, improve the quality of life and boost the local economy.

Soft Power

Power (of a nation, state, alliance, etc.) deriving from economic and cultural influence, rather than coercion or military strength; cf. hard power...

Ubiquitous City As South Korea's early version of the smart city concept, it was also called U-city. U-city was defined as a city that fused high-tech infrastructure and ubiquitous information service into the urban area, enabling services such as a one-stop administration service, automatic traffic, crime prevention, and home networking of residential places.

Virtual Reality The computer-generated simulation of a three-dimensional image or environment that enables users to explore and interact with a virtual surrounding.

HISTORICAL TIMELINE OF SOUTH KOREA AND THE CITY OF SEOUL

2333BC   The first Korean kingdom, 'Gojoseon,' is established on the Korean peninsula.

372   Three kingdoms (Goguryeo, Shilla, and Baekje) rule over the Korean peninsula.

676   Shilla unites three kingdoms.

918   Koryo Dynasty is established.

1392   Joseon is established.

1394   Seoul becomes the Joseon capital.

1443   Hangul is created by King Sejong.

1905   Korea becomes a protectorate of the Empire of Japan under Japan-Korea Treaty.

1910   The Empire of Japan annexes Korea.

1945   World War II ends with Japan's defeat, and Korea is liberated from Japan.

1946   The first mayor of Seoul is assigned by the US Military Government.

1948   Two separate governments are formed in the Korean Peninsula: The socialist government in the North and the capitalist government in the South.

The first presidential election is held in the South, and Rhee Syngman becomes the first president of the Republic of Korea.

Seoul officially becomes the capital of South Korea.

1950   The Korean War breaks out

1953   An armistice agreement is reached on July 27, 1953, ending the Korean War.

1960   The April Revolution erupts, and President Rhee Syngman steps down.

1961   Military coup puts General Park Chung-hee in power.

1962   The Korean government establishes the Urban Planning Act.

Seoul government starts to set up urban master plans and development projects for city planning.

1969   The Cheonggye Elevated Motorway opens.

1970   South Korea's exports surpass US$1 billion.

1972   Park Chung-hee enacts the Yushin Order.

1974   Seoul Metropolitan Subway begins operations.

1979   Park is assassinated and General Chun Doo-hwan seizes power.

1980   The Gwangju Uprising is put down by Chun's military regime.

1983   The Han River Development Plan is announced.

1986   The Asian Games are held in Seoul.

1987   The June Democracy Movement forces Chun to call elections for the presidency and the local governors.

1988   The Olympic Games are held in Seoul.
Seoul's population exceeds 10 million.

1994   The Seongsu Bridge disaster kills 32 people.

1995   South Korea holds the first election of provincial and municipal officials since the May 16 coup of 1961. Cho Soon is elected Mayor of Seoul.

The Sampoong Department Store collapse kills over 500 people.

1996	South Korea is admitted as a member of the Organization for Economic Cooperation and Development (OECD).
1997	The IMF crisis plunges the Korean economy into recession. Korea receives a US$36 billion recovery loan.
1998	Goh Kun becomes the 2nd Mayor of Seoul.
2001	South Korea repays the IMF in full ahead of time.
2002	South Korea holds the 17th FIFA World Cup along with Japan, and the Korean team reaches the semi-finals. Lee Myung-bak becomes the 3rd Mayor of Seoul.
2004	Seoul implements the public transport system reform with BRT lines and smart cards.
2005	The restored Cheonggyecheon opens to the public.
2006	Oh Se-hoon becomes the 4th Mayor of Seoul and announces the Han River Renaissance Project.
2007	The Seoul government announces The SHIFT program for equitable housing.
2008	The Seoul Public Design Guidelines are announced.
2009	Moonlight Rainbow Fountain installed.
2010	The city of Seoul is designated as 'the UNESCO Creative City for Design.'
2011	Park Won-soon becomes the 5th Mayor of Seoul
2012	Seoul's data portal website 'Open Data Plaza' opens.
2014	Dongdaemun Design Plaza opens to the Public. Inaugural opening of Sebitseom takes place.

2015   Seoul launches 'Ddareungi,' the public bike-sharing program.

The Park administration establishes Seoul Urban Solutions Agency (SUSA).

2017   'Seoullo7017,' known as the Seoul Skypark, opens to the public.

Seoul launches 'Nanumcar,' Seoul's public car-sharing platform.

The Digital Mayor's Office service launches.

2021   Oh Se-hoon is re-elected Mayor of Seoul.

REFERENCES FOR SEOUL RESEARCH

Websites

1. Beautiful Foundation. (n.d.). Retrieved from https://beautifulfund.org/

2. CityNet Secretariat. (n.d.). CityNet Secretariat. Retrieved from https://citynet-ap.org/

3. FIWARE – Open APIs for Open Minds. (n.d.). Retrieved from https://www.fiware.org/

4. Korea Agency for Infrastructure Technology Advancement. (n.d.). Retrieved from https://www.kaia.re.kr/

5. Korea International Cooperation Agency. (n.d.). Retrieved from http://www.koica.go.kr/

6. Korea Overseas Infrastructure & Urban Development Corporation. (n.d.). Retrieved from http://www.kindkorea.or.kr/

7. Korea's Smart City Portal. (n.d.). Retrieved from https://smartcity.go.kr/

8. National Museum Of Korean Contemporary History. (n.d.). Retrieved from https://www.much.go.kr/en

9. Official website of SOCAR. (n.d.). Retrieved from https://www.socar.kr/

10. People's Solidarity for Participatory Democracy. (n.d.). Retrieved from https://www.peoplepower21.org/category/english

11. Seoul Design Foundation. (n.d.). Retrieved from https://seouldesign.or.kr/

12. Seoul Metropolitan Government. (n.d.). Retrieved from https://english.seoul.go.kr/

13. Seoul Museum of History. (n.d.). Retrieved from https://museum.seoul.go.kr/

14. Seoul Open Data Plaza. (n.d.). Retrieved from https://data.seoul.go.kr/

15. Seoul Research Data Service. (n.d.). Retrieved from https://data.si.re.kr/

16. Seoul Share Hub. (n.d.). Retrieved from http://sharehub.kr/

17. Seoul Solution. (n.d.). Retrieved from https://seoulsolution.kr/

18. Seoul Urban Solutions Agency. (n.d.). Retrieved from https://www.susa.or.kr/en

19. South Korea Presidential Archives. (n.d.). Retrieved from https://www.pa.go.kr

20. South Korea Public Data Portal. (n.d.). Retrieved from https://www.data.go.kr/

21. WeGO: World Smart Cities Organization. (n.d.). Retrieved from https://we-gov.org

Books, Articles and More

1. Magazine-B (2018). Issue No. 50, Seoul. Second Edition. Brand Documentary Magazine.

2. Breen, M. (2017). The New Koreans: The Business, History and People of South Korea. Rider Press Ltd.

3. Brossa Balcells, M. (2019). Building an architecture of everyday life in South Korea: Mass housing estates in Seoul as an instrument of modernization, 1962-2008. Universitat Politècnica de Catalunya. Escola Tècnica Superior d'Arquitectura de Barcelona.

4. Busquets, J. (2011). Deconstruction/construction: The Cheonggyecheon Restoration Project in Seoul. Harvard Univ Graduate School of.

5. Cha, V. & Pacheco Pardo, R. (2023). Korea: A New History of South & North. Yale University Press.

6. Cheonggyecheon Museum. (2016). Cheonggyecheon: Flowing Through Seoul and Reflecting Seoul's History.

7. Cindy Loffler, S. (2020, April 7). The mayor of Seoul rolls out a smart city. https://www.ces.tech/articles/2020/the-mayor-of-seoul-rolls-out-a-smart-city.aspx

8. Eckert, C. (2016). Park Chung Hee and Modern Korea. The Belknap Press of Harvard University Press.

9. Flynn, L. (2023). The 20 richest cities in the world. Money Inc. https://moneyinc.com/richest-cities-in-the-world-in-2022/

10. Foucault, M. (2007). Discipline and Punish. In Duke University Press eBooks (pp. 444–471). https://doi.org/10.1215/9780822390169-018

11. Grimaldi, D., & Carrasco-Farré, C. (2021). Implementing Data-Driven Strategies in Smart Cities: A Roadmap for Urban Transformation. Elsevier.

12. Harvard University Graduate School of Design. (2021, January 28). Veronica Rudge Green Prize in Urban Design – Harvard Graduate School of Design. https://www.gsd.harvard.edu/urban-planning-design/fellowships-prizes-and-travel-programs/veronica-rudge-green-prize-in-urban-design/

13. Heroes of the Environment – TIME. (2007, October 17). TIME.com. http://content.time.com/time/specials/2007/article/0,28804,1663317_1663319_1669884,00.html

14. Interview with Seoul Mayor Oh Se-hoon. (2022, December 2). [Video]. YouTube. https://www.youtube.com/watch?v=yi2cIvRyPVc

15. Kim, P., & Vogel, E. F. (2011). The Park Chung Hee Era: The Transformation of South Korea. In Harvard University Press eBooks. https://doi.org/10.4159/harvard.9780674061064

16. Lee, Y. (2014). New Dawn: Republic of Korea and Syngman Rhee. Createspace Independent Publishing Platform.

17. Lessig, L. (2009). Remix: making art and commerce thrive in the hybrid economy. Choice Reviews Online, 46(09), 46–5102. https://doi.org/10.5860/choice.46-5102

18. McLaren, D., & Agyeman, J. (2015). Sharing Cities: A Case for Truly Smart and Sustainable Cities. MIT Press.

19. MOLIT & KAIA. (2021). Smart City TOP Agenda: Smart City Global Journal.

20. Pyoang-Guk, K. E. V. F. (2014). The Park Chung Hee Era: The Transformation of South Korea. Harvard University Press.

21. Rifkin, J. (2001). The Age of Access: How the Shift from Ownership to Access is Transforming Modern Life.

22. Robinson, T., & Ji, M. (2022). Sustainable, smart and solidary Seoul: Transforming an Asian Megacity. Springer Nature.

23. Seoul Design Foundation. (2015). The story of dreaming, creating and enjoying DDP.

24. Seoul Design Foundation. (2017). Dream.Design.Play. Dongdaemun Design Plaza.

25. Seoul Smart City White Paper: Smart City Manual for Citizens and Mayor. (2019). Seoul Metropolitan Government.

26. Tudor, D. (2012). Korea: The Impossible Country. Tuttle Publishing.

27. United Nations E-Government Survey 2022. (2022). https://doi.org/10.18356/9789210019446

Acknowledgments

Thanks to Dr. Song Kuk-jin and Lee Kyungwoo for not only introducing us, but also inspiring us with their kindness and goodwill.

Thanks to subject matter experts in transport Min Jaehong, Dr. Cho Shin-Hyung and Lee Seung-ha for taking the time out of their busy schedules to advise us on the transport chapters of this book. And thanks to the Digital Mayor's Office expert Cho Yong-hyun for his patient explanations of the project and a very cool demo of how it works. A special thanks to our subject matter expert in data science, Dr. Hwang Jong-Sung, for advising us on our data science chapter as well as the overall structure of the book, and for always being such a lively and interesting interview subject. Also thanks to former Ambassador Choi Seokyoung for his input on the development of Seoul over the past 30 years. We would also like to extend our heartfelt appreciation to Seoul's Senior Policy Advisor, Lee Kwang-seok, for generously dedicating his time to impart his knowledge and experiences regarding Seoul's recent history of urban development policies and for reviewing our manuscript.

To our proofreaders, Anne-Sophie Mahle, Dr. Kim Heeju, Professor Oh Daniel, Chun Julie Hyo Jin, Kim Junsung and Dr. Didier Grimaldi for their time and valuable feedback. It means so much to us.

Also thanks to Han Sunjung of the Han Youngsoo Foundation for allowing us to use one of Han Youngsoo's photos of Seoul in the 1950s. It is an honor for us to be able to include one of these pieces that allow us a glimpse of Seoul before the Miracle began. Also a special thanks to Lina Lee for her painting of the Seoul landscape.

And most importantly, thanks to Domingo, Alex, Sharol, Juan, Woo-bin and the LGU+ smart city team members for all of their love and support during this process.

About Atmosphere Press

Founded in 2015, Atmosphere Press was built on the principles of Honesty, Transparency, Professionalism, Kindness, and Making Your Book Awesome. As an ethical and author-friendly hybrid press, we stay true to that founding mission today.

If you're a reader, enter our giveaway for a free book here:

SCAN TO ENTER
BOOK GIVEAWAY

If you're a writer, submit your manuscript for consideration here:

SCAN TO SUBMIT
MANUSCRIPT

And always feel free to visit Atmosphere Press and our authors online at atmospherepress.com. See you there soon!

About the Authors

DR. SUNG-JIN PARK is an industry expert at LGU+ specializing in smart cities and has a two-decade career in this field. Her journey commenced as a city planner at the Incheon Institute, where she honed her skills and expertise. After earning her Ph.D. in urban planning and policy at the University of California, Irvine, in the United States, she embarked on an eight-year tenure with Samsung SDS, serving as an IT consultant with a specialization in the execution of various smart city consulting and implementation projects. In 2021, Dr. Park made the transition to the LGU+ smart city team, dedicating two years to innovating services for Sejong National Pilot City, a prominent initiative in South Korea. She has closely collaborated with both private and public sectors, making significant contributions to the development of a wide array of smart city projects leveraging cutting-edge technologies.

KRISTI SHALLA is a Senior Smart City Consultant with 15 years of development experience in the US, Europe and the APAC region. She is an expert in global economic development and building innovative ecosystems and currently holds the position of Innovation Commissioner at the Embassy of Switzerland in Washington, DC. Before relocating to Washington, DC, in the fall of 2020, Kristi was Head of Project Development at the Center for Innovation in Transport (CENIT) in Barcelona, Spain, where she built public and private partnerships in transport and smart city research for projects around the globe, including extensive work in South Korea. She also spent ten years in New York City working with the Singaporean and Hong Kong governments. Kristi has over 15 years experience in building development projects between the US, Europe and the APAC region. Kristi is an experienced speaker, lecturer and contributor on the topic of urban mobility, smart city development and international expansion.